Sassy Planet

Sassy Planet

A QUEER GUIDE TO 40 CITIES, BIG AND SMALL

Harish Bhandari, David Dodge, and Nick Schiarizzi
Illustrated by Bráulio Amado

PRESTEL
MUNICH · LONDON · NEW YORK

C O N T

E N T S

AFRICA

ASIA

AUSTRALIA

Introduction

For decades, LGBTQ travelers have congregated in predictable places: queer-friendly cities like New York and Berlin, or secluded beach towns such as Mykonos and Fire Island. We've stuck to this same fruit-loop of destinations for the opportunity—still rare for so many of us—to be around large groups of other gay, lesbian, bisexual, or transgender people. We've also done this for a less sexy reason: safety. Same-sex sexual acts are still illegal in over 70 countries, and punishable by death in at least 12. Even where queerness is legal, we are often the targets of violence and harassment.

But acceptance in cities and countries around the world is also on the rise, creating new, exciting destinations ready for LGBTQ folks to enjoy (if we can get past our preconception of what a "gay" travel destination looks like). As queer progress and visibility expands, so do our travel options. Rather than escaping to gay ghettos like New York's West Village or San Francisco's Castro at the first opportunity, more people are staying put in their hometowns or moving to smaller cities and areas not typically thought of as LGBTQ-friendly. Others are pioneering queer communities on the fringes of the larger cities we already know and love. As a result, vibrant, surprising scenes are being established all over the world—and we want to shine a big gay spotlight on some of them for the first time.

This book aims to do exactly that: we've found, explored, and documented cool queer shit happening in cities of all sizes. And we've been able to do this thanks to the biggest advantage gay travelers have over our straight counterparts: tried-and-true "hookup" apps. It turns out they're not only about sex—they can also serve as global libraries of people and communities who share our minority status. In addition to anonymous chats, we've also reached out to many prominent queer people worldwide to gain their perspectives on the LGBTQ scenes in their respective cities.

The idea for *Sassy Planet* was inspired by our alternative travel website, forbottoms.com, where we chat with locals through Grindr, Scruff, and other apps to discover interesting things— nightlife, art, culture, history, and more—in cities across the world, and then write about it all. The name *For Bottoms* is a jab at how subdivided our community can be: bears, otters, twinks, muscle queens, Solange fans … it's as if you'd need your own special gay guide based on your preferred sexual position. The astute homo may pick up on a little pun in there too: some of the places we profile on the site are literally at the "bottom" of the list for most gay travelers. But hopefully not for long.

Lastly, it's worth noting that we didn't start this project amid a global pandemic—but we certainly ended it in one. We want to recognize that a large proportion of our global LGBTQ community is employed in many of the industries hit hardest by the economic fallout from Covid-19: nightlife, hospitality, tourism, art, and more. Many of the people you will read about in this book have had their careers—and lives—put on hold due to quarantines and lockdowns. Some of the nightclubs and parties you'll read about may no longer exist; many of the artists and performers are out of jobs. We encourage you to find these venues and artists online and support them in any way you can.

Pandemic aside, this book is nonetheless the culmination of several years of work to bring the concept of our website to the printed page. It illuminates what's new and emerging in LGBTQ spaces around the world and serves as a snapshot of queer life at this very crazy, very queer moment in time.

This is *Sassy Planet*.

North

Austin, Texas

When asked where the gayborhood is in Austin, most locals will say it's literally everywhere. This city is so LGBTQ-friendly that a traditional gay ghetto doesn't really exist; instead the scene spreads its super-queer tentacles into almost every area. Austin is *so* gay, in fact, that it holds not one Pride event each summer, but two: an official one in August, and an anti-corporate protest called QueerBomb that takes over the streets in June.

A Guide to Austin's Gay, Gay Neighborhoods

Locals say Austin has no single queer neighborhood. Each area of the city has its own vibe, which Austinites describe thusly:

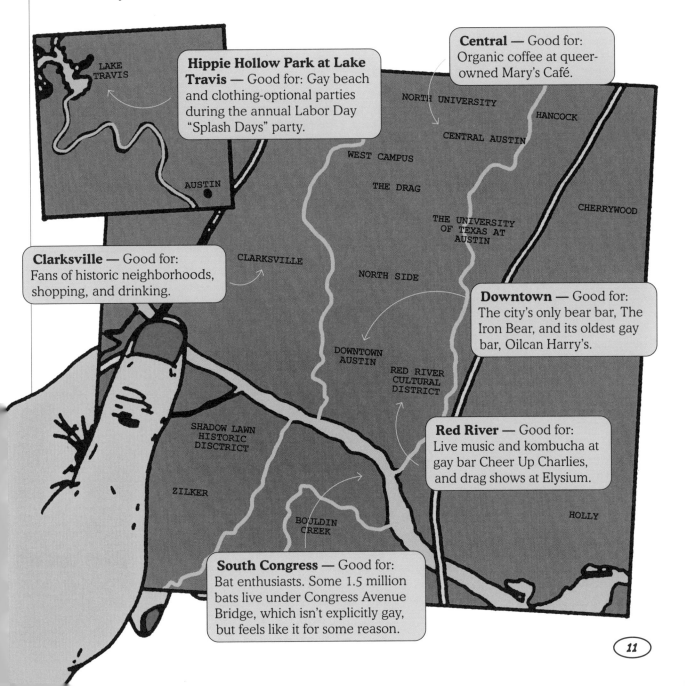

Central — Good for: Organic coffee at queer-owned Mary's Café.

Hippie Hollow Park at Lake Travis — Good for: Gay beach and clothing-optional parties during the annual Labor Day "Splash Days" party.

Clarksville — Good for: Fans of historic neighborhoods, shopping, and drinking.

Downtown — Good for: The city's only bear bar, The Iron Bear, and its oldest gay bar, Oilcan Harry's.

Red River — Good for: Live music and kombucha at gay bar Cheer Up Charlies, and drag shows at Elysium.

South Congress — Good for: Bat enthusiasts. Some 1.5 million bats live under Congress Avenue Bridge, which isn't explicitly gay, but feels like it for some reason.

Map labels: LAKE TRAVIS, AUSTIN, NORTH UNIVERSITY, HANCOCK, CENTRAL AUSTIN, WEST CAMPUS, THE DRAG, CHERRYWOOD, THE UNIVERSITY OF TEXAS AT AUSTIN, CLARKSVILLE, NORTH SIDE, DOWNTOWN AUSTIN, RED RIVER CULTURAL DISTRICT, SHADOW LAWN HISTORIC DISCTRICT, ZILKER, BOULDIN CREEK, HOLLY

Double Scorpio: Austin's Home-Grown "VHS Cleaner"

In 2017, Julian Eternal, a gay who hails from Upstate New York, co-founded Double Scorpio with his boyfriend. The brand sells what we're all just going to collectively agree to call "VHS cleaners" from this point forward. Julian didn't set out to be the queer cleaner mogul of Austin. In fact, he was specifically drawn to the city for what he describes as its "wonderful slacker mentality."

"No one I knew at the time had a job," he says. This was made possible by the city's low cost of living—rent in Julian's first apartment was just $200 a month. "We used to say that Austin is where young people go to retire," he adds. That version of Austin, he explains wistfully, is no longer. Rents in some areas are now comparable to Los Angeles, since the tech industry is booming and attracting new blood to the city. "Today it's not hard to find, like, a 25-year-old queer guy who is super goal-oriented and lives in a condo," he says.

Julian may not live in a condo, but a chance experience several years ago would eventually turn him, too, into an ambitious homosexual entrepreneur. After trying a different brand of, *ahem*, cleaner (shoved under his nose while at a party in New Orleans), he came back to Austin with a painful and unsightly burn. He and his boyfriend, a neuroscientist, quickly made it their mission to concoct a version of a cleaner that wouldn't, as Julian puts it, "burn your fucking face off."

And thus, after channeling their inner Beaker the Muppet for several months, Double Scorpio was born (yes, both Julian and his boyfriend are Scorpios). At first, Julian planned to make the cleaner just for his personal use, and to maybe sell a bottle here and there to friends and other cleaner enthusiasts. "We honestly didn't do this to make any money, but it just kind of took off," he

(1)

says. "I was really surprised how excited people in Austin were for something like this. Next thing I knew we were doing pop-up shops in bars, where people would stop by just to buy a shirt."

After developing a devoted customer base (which includes *RuPaul's Drag Race* alum Willam, who reached out to Julian to collaborate on some

---

1: Double Scorpio co-founder Julian Eternal. Opposite: *Drag Race* alum Willam's collaboration with the brand.

(1)

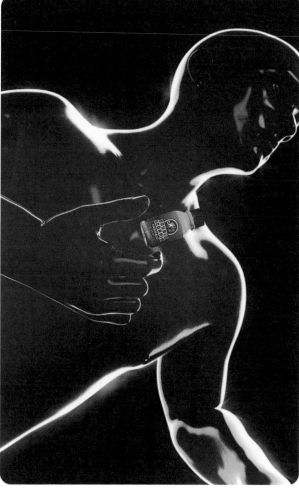

(2)

merchandise), Double Scorpio began to venture into non-cleaner territory, making jockstraps, shirts, and, perhaps an obvious route, throwing queer raves. Julian had long been a fan of the dance music scene in San Francisco and hoped to bring a bit of that energy to Austin, which he describes as having been "very vanilla" when he first moved there. "Our first party was in a CrossFit gym that we totally transformed into a rave space, with professional lighting, sound, and of course a darkroom," he recalls. "We had some pretty cool DJs at that first party, like Octo Octa."

Julian was unsure at first whether people in Austin would embrace a San Francisco vibe, but the parties took off. His most recent event sold 700 tickets and was a fully realized gay party.

As he explains, "People couldn't even get into the darkroom, it was so crowded—the queers in Austin were clearly hungry for something like this!"

Julian is particularly proud of the crowd he cultivates at these parties. "It's really integrated," he says. "In some cities you go to a queer rave and it's usually all white cis men, but that doesn't really exist in Austin."

1 & 2: Double Scorpio VHS cleaner advertisements.

Julian Eternal's
Top Austin To-Dos for Ho-Mos

Coconut Club

"This was started by two bartenders who worked at an old gay bar that's closed now, but which really defined my first few years in Austin. It's good dance music, almost a lesbian bar, very quintessentially queer Austin."

Rain on 4th and Oilcan Harry's

"These are the Top 40s bars everyone makes fun of but still goes to."

QueerBomb

"This is Austin's alternative queer pride; it's more of a protest. It was started basically as a response to the fact that the regular Pride is super corporate."

Chicago, Illinois

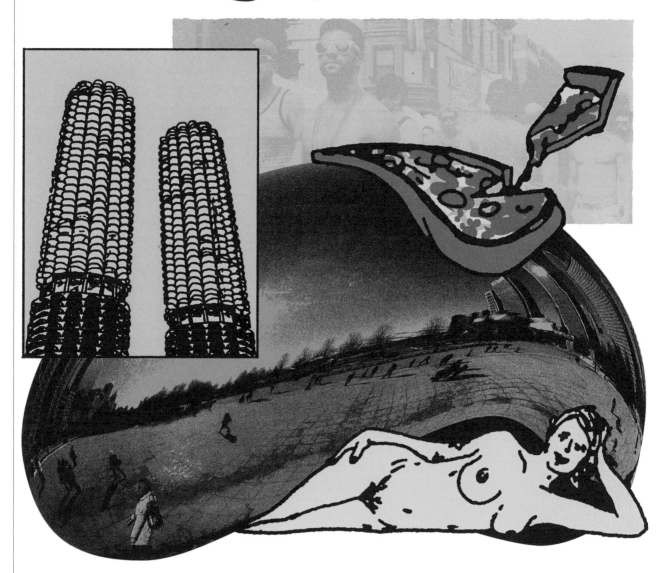

In 1924 a gay soldier named Henry Gerber, fresh from an army deployment in Germany where he learned of the pioneering work of sexologist Magnus Hirschfeld, founded the Society for Human Rights in Chicago—the first queer rights organization in the United States. American society wasn't quite ready for what Gerber had to say, and sadly the group lasted only a few years. However, the groundwork was laid, and Chicago's place in American queerstory was firmly established.

These days, Chicago, with its massive skyline hugging a lake the size of a small sea, is a city quietly confident of its place in the world. Although oft overlooked by international tourists, it becomes a playground in summer, hosting more major LGBTQ festivals than New York City.

Chat WITH A LOCAL

Sassy_Planet: House music is one of Chicago's most famous exports. How integral is it to the LGBTQ scene and culture of the city these days?

BillyP: House music exploded in the 1980s, roughly 40 years ago. While there are still a handful of LGBTQ parties and one-off events on holiday weekends, it's a smaller scene. Queen! at Smartbar is a true house music party with great DJs. Bars that cater to younger crowds play pop and hip-hop—it's very much a generational thing.

Sassy_Planet: How was the house music scene a part of your own coming up and coming out process?

BillyP: If you grew up in Chicago during the '80s, you grew up with house music. Every Friday and Saturday night, the entire city was tuned in to either the WBMX or WGCI radio stations to hear hours of live mixes from the pioneering DJs that also played at clubs around the city. Every car radio was tuned in at the same time, so you would literally hear it everywhere if you were out and about.

BillyP: Some of the DJs would take more chances and play a lot of Italo disco and European dance records in addition to new US-based tracks—from homegrown labels like Trax and DJ International, and hundreds of smaller ones. It was only when you left Chicago that you realized that we were the only ones who knew these records— and we eventually realized how electrifying and unique that time was in our city.

Sassy_Planet: Were the '80s a unique moment, with straight and non-straight people in Chicago listening to the exact same music?

BillyP: To a large degree, yes, especially among the Black community. However, there were also a lot of new wave and pop-progressive scenes with a mostly white clientele, where European commercial music prevailed.

Sassy_Planet: Given Chicago's unique history, the importance of house music in the queer world, and the fact that it's the third-largest US city, it's sometimes surprising that more LGBTQ travelers don't include it on their itineraries. What do you think Chicago has to offer?

BillyP: Chicago is a unique blend that captures a bit of both NYC and San Francisco: sprawling, iconic architecture, museums, theater, and countless cultural institutions, alongside a beautiful blue backyard—one of the world's largest sources of fresh water, Lake Michigan. The food and dining scene here is also legendary, as are the many neighborhoods that charm the most jaded of visitors. If you're coming to party for IML (International Mr. Leather), Midsommarfest, Pride Fest, or Market Days, you'll have a blast—but your trip will be more memorable if you dig in and live like a local.

Market Days.

Honolulu, Hawaii

B ack in 1993, Honolulu definitely wasn't seen as a bastion of LGBTQ rights or activism. But all that changed suddenly when the Supreme Court of Hawaii took on a case involving three same-sex couples hoping to marry in the state that year. The court decided that, in not allowing them to marry, the law might be discriminating against the couples on the basis of their sexuality. The groundbreaking ruling suddenly bolstered hope nationwide that the US government would finally begin to grant a new set of rights to queer couples.

Over the next several years, however, the ruling was kept in limbo, tossed around courts and in state government, with hopes rising and falling in the process. Bill Clinton put the kibosh on the situation by signing the Defense of Marriage Act in 1996, banning gay marriage on a federal level. External funding from elsewhere in the US, such as anti-gay Christian organizations, also helped to tamp down the initial excitement from the 1993 ruling. It additionally influenced the passage of Hawaii's Constitutional Amendment 2 in 1998, which gave the state legislature the power to ban gay marriage—which it did soon after.

Gay marriage did not become legal in Hawaii until 2013, but in the process of bringing the issue to the courts, the chambers of legislature, and the voting booths over the course of the 1990s, the state became a testing ground for the advancement of LGBTQ Americans' legal rights. These days, Honolulu's gay footprint can be felt more on the shores of Waikiki than at the state's high court just across town. The scene here is small, friendly, and different from anything else you'll experience on the US mainland.

Dustin Koda Spills His GUTS

Dustin Koda is a designer, DJ, and party promoter who was born and bred in Hawaii. He co-founded the queer media company GUTS NYC, a site and app that impressively and exhaustively aggregated all of the many, many queer happenings in New York City. In 2018, after a 14-year stint in New York, Dustin returned to his homeland, where he's been plotting all the ways to queer up Honolulu using the skills he honed in the Big Apple.

Sassy Planet: Who are you, Dustin?
Dustin Koda: I'm Dustin Koda, aka DJ Dust Blaze, and I was born and raised in Hawaii. I moved to NYC in 2004 but returned to Hawaii in 2018. I don't know if you've seen the movie *Brooklyn*, but it's perfectly descriptive of someone having two homes and thus having two very separate and distinct lives. The duality in spatial identification [in the film] felt painfully resonant to me.

When I was in NYC I lived in 10 different places that spanned Queens, Brooklyn, and Manhattan. I DJed and had parties at [queer venues] The Cock, Nowhere Bar, and 3 Dollar Bill. I developed an app with my partner that was a wayfinding platform that identified every NYC gay institution, from [queer health center] Callen-Lorde to sex shops, and every bar and club, which I individually solicited and visited—so I'm very familiar with everything NYC had to offer.

NYC, which has become increasingly unaffordable, slowly pushed me out, and I found myself back in Hawaii with ambitions to give back to the place that had fostered my growth.

SP: What's been your personal contribution to the LGBTQ community in Honolulu?
DK: To just exist as I am feels at odds with the prevalent attitudes and politics of what does occasionally feel like a small town. Everything I participate in flows from that attitude as a provocateur, like throwing my party GUTS or DJing.

I plan on continuing to facilitate queer-oriented spaces and events that are driven by cultural themes rather than being primarily just homo-centric. I'm trying to foster the creative spirit that was so abundant when I was in my twenties.

SP: Does Honolulu have something special to offer a queer visitor?

DK: Hawaii was one of the first states to bring talks of civil unions to the table, and it's generally a solidly blue state. But when it came to enacting gay marriage laws, we were really cockblocked by religious fundamentalists—even though Hawaii's native *aikāne* [gay] and *Māhū* [trans or third sex] cultures were inclusive toward gay people, who even held their own special place in society. [Compared to when] I left in 2004 there seems to be a very apparent deficiency of 20-to-30-somethings, who probably all moved to more urban centers, thus making Hawaii less gay. You've probably heard of the phenomenon not-so-nicely named "brain drain" and its effects on smaller cities. That, compounded with Hawaii's extremely remote location, dissuades potential visitors who want to vacation somewhere warm, and they'll most likely opt for someplace cheaper and in closer proximity instead. Hawaii is unique in so many ways; it really has no peer. It's heavily influenced not only by its native culture but also by its Asian and Portuguese settlers.

SP: In smaller cities there tends to be a melding of subgroups (twinks, bears, and so on into one big group, so that all different types of LGBTQ people hang in the same few spaces. Is this the case in Honolulu?

DK: There are no incredibly diverse groups of queers in Hawaii. Since there aren't as many queer residents, the distinguishing identifications are much broader. People usually group themselves by age, then whether you are a "townie" (Honolulu resident) versus people who live on the west side of the island ("country"). There's also a contingency of military gays, who do have a strong tendency to stick among themselves. Ethnically, Hawaii is tremendously mixed and diverse, so that plays a significantly smaller role here than in other cities.

SP: Is there any interesting Hawaiian gay folklore or mythology? And what about cruising zones?

DK: An umbrella term, *Māhū*, has recently come to identify more of our trans population. Since the advent of Grindr and Scruff, cruising spots like Queens Beach, Video Warehouse, Max's Gym, and P10A have all really vanished. There's a beach on the North Shore that's generally—though not legally—for nudists, but it's also where a lot of queer and trans people feel safe to congregate.

SP: Does being in Hawaii allow for a special mindset that sets it apart from the mainland USA in terms of the queer racism issues that are typically rampant (especially on hookup apps)?

DK: Even though Hawaii is racially diverse we're still subject to American media and colonial influence, and white features are often valued above others.

Growing up, I had less of a sense of being non-Caucasian than I would've had if I'd grown up in any other state, but gay culture still often feels racist—more so in the townie spheres than in the country, which is perceived as being more "local" and less *haole*. *Haole* is defined as "foreigner" but has significant overlap with being white. But you can be white and not act *haole*, which is more descriptive of a sense of entitlement and a disregard for the ways our local culture operates. So while not all white people act *haole*, almost all *haoles* are white, because it's that demographic that tends to arrive with the expectation that the world will bend to their standards.

It was very interesting that when I was in New York, the thing I primarily identified with was being "of Hawaii" (not "Hawaiian," which is an ethnic—and not particularly a cultural—distinction). Now that I'm here in Honolulu again, it means very little to have an identity primarily founded on something that we all are, so I've reverted back to being the "alternative" or "urban" person—whereas in NYC, everyone was necessarily urban, and alternative thinkers have a tendency to gravitate there. I was always both of those things, but, like anything, your differences tend to become your characterizing attributes.

Dustin Koda's
Top Honolulu To-Dos
for Ho-Mos

Polo Beach

"A gay-friendly beach on the North Shore—but really, any beach on the North Shore is worth a gander."

Ala Moana Center

"Mall with a lot of stores that you won't find anywhere else in the state."

Thrift shopping

"Savers or Goodwill might be a fun experience for visitors, who may enjoy the novelty of finding things that are uniquely common to Hawaii, like Aloha shirts."

Downtown Honolulu

"Downtown Honolulu and the Kaka'ako neighborhood, where you have a lot of artisanal goods and restaurants, are the hip places right now."

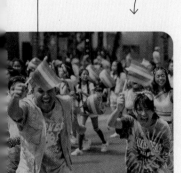

Waikiki

"Often thought of as a tourist trap—but it's where most of the gay businesses are, so if a visitor wants to find a hookup or just a safe space for queers, they'll likely be spending some time in Waikiki (which does have its own idyllic charm)."

Kansas City, Missouri

The queer scene in Kansas City, Missouri, is small but mighty—visitors are often surprised to learn just how vibrant and diverse it is. Care to try your hand (or legs) at line dancing with a handsome stranger? Sidekicks Saloon has got you covered. Want to pretend to watch a Royals game while cruising with a beer in hand? Head on down to Woody's. Itching to catch a cabaret show with bearded drag queens and Bruno Mars-impersonating drag kings? Missie B's is the place to be. Not into nightlife, but really into fountains? KC's got over 200, which is pretty gay.

Kansas City Activist Keith Spare

Keith Spare, a 71-year-old gay rights activist, first moved to Kansas City in 1967 as, in his words, a "bright-eyed, brown-haired kid from Brown County, Kansas." Early on, he happened upon the Phoenix Society, the city's first gay rights organization. "It gave me a whole new outlook on life," he says.

Keith began to cautiously dip his toe into advocacy with the group, but he understandably —this being 1960s Missouri—didn't have plans to come out too publicly. However, after a conference he was helping to quietly organize at Kent State University listed him as part of the "Gay Liberation Movement" in its program (which was subsequently passed out to faculty and students across campus), he figured there wasn't much point in hiding any longer. "So I came out like Evel Knievel in a cannon," he says.

Freed from the closet, Keith doubled down on his activism work with the Phoenix Society. In 1966 he helped to organize a meeting with members of the North American Conference of Homophile Organizations, thought to be the first ever public gathering of gay and lesbian groups in the country. And he helped put out *The Phoenix*, a newsletter that published artwork, articles, poetry, and news about the Kansas City LGBTQ community. "It was a well-put-together publication, particularly for the time, and was really well read," Keith explains. "It became a great way to show how vibrant and connected our community was."

Looking back on this time, Keith says he's impressed by the progress that Kansas City has made in the years since. "It's amazing how far we've come," he says, noting the city's annual Pride festivities as a prime example. "There's so much more diversity today; all of the letters in our acronym are represented. I can't imagine where we'll be in another 10 years."

(1)   (2)

(3)

1: May 19, 1990: Keith Spare becomes the first openly gay Methodist to graduate from the United Methodist Church Seminary. 2 & 3: The February 1968 issue of Kansas City LGBTQ advocacy magazine *The Phoenix*.

Queer History:

KANSAS CITY, HOME TO THE FIRST HOMO CONFERENCE

On February 18, 1966, a group of 14 LGBTQ rights groups from around the United States traveled to Kansas City to take part in the first meeting of the North American Conference of Homophile Organizations (NACHO, pronounced Nay-Ko). Although the alliance was short-lived—NACHO held just two more conferences before disbanding soon after the Stonewall Riots in 1969 sparked a new generation of activism—the gathering has gone down in history as the first ever public meeting of "homophile" organizations in the country.

Midwest Homophile Conference in Kansas City

A Midwest Regional Homophile ...ference will meet in Kansas City ...ebruary 23-25 at the invitation ...Phoenix Society. Dallas, Cincia-... and Chicago are expected to ...nd delegates to the meeting. At ...ss time it was not known if the ...mophile organizations in Denver, ...troit, and Rock Island, Illinois, ...ould be represented. At least one ...bserver is expected, Miss Shirley ...iller, national president of the ...aughters of Bilitis.

The high point of the conference ...ill be a public meeting on "The ...oral Aspects of the Gay Person in ...Straight Society." This will be a panel discussion led by Paul Jones, associate professor of philosophical theology at St. Paul School of Theology. Leaders of several bo-mophile organizations will sit on the panel, and time will be alotted for questions from the audience. The open meeting will be held at 8:00 pm, Saturday, February 24, at the Center for Renewal, St. Paul School of Theology, 1525 Denver St.

The conference will open Friday

evening with a welcoming supper at 7:00 pm. At 10:00 pm several dele-gates will speak on Steve Boll's radio show, "Assignment Kansas City," on KMBZ.

Business sessions will open at 9:00 am and will last until 5:00 pm, with a noon - time break for lunch. The Conference Dinner will be held at 5:30 at a popular K. C. restaurant.

After the 8:00 public meeting men-tioned above, bar tours will be con-ducted for those delegates who are interested. A send - off brunch at 11:00 am Sunday will close the con-ference.

Planning of the conference has been in the hands of Vaun Anderson and Marc Jeffers, respectively con-ference chairman and secretary. Es-telle Graham is directing the social activities, and other Phoenix mem-bers are assisting in numerous ways.

4

City of Fountains

Kansas City is known as the "City of Fountains," with more than 200 of the water-bearing structures spread across the municipality. The city even honors this nickname with an official holiday each April, when its infamous aquatic shooters gloriously erupt once again after many months of abstinence each winter. Here are some of KC's queerest fountains:

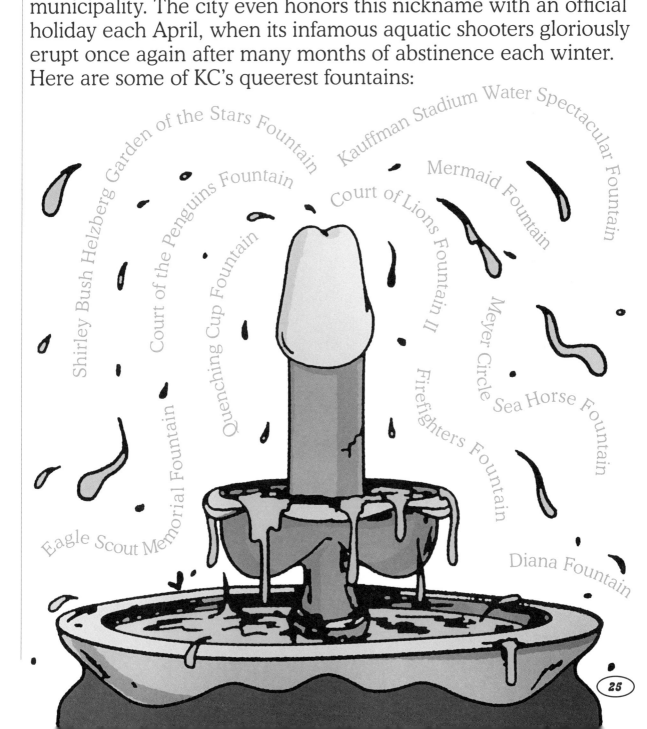

Mexico City, Mexico

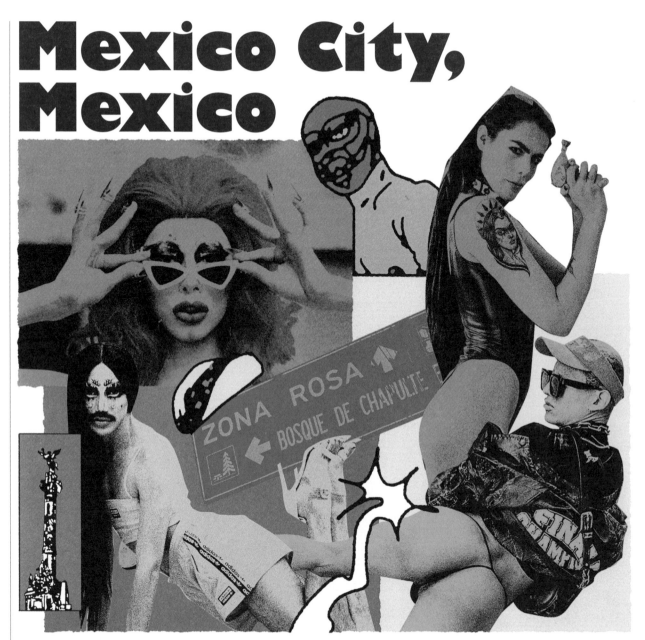

You're probably tired of hearing about Mexico City—it's one of those places your friends visit and then won't shut up about. Eventually you end up in Ciudad de Mexico (Mexico City, or CDMX) for one reason or another, and it not only lives up to the hype, it turns you into a Mexico Motormouth too. Upon arrival, LGBTQ visitors can marvel at the openness of gay couples holding hands in the Zona Rosa ("Pink Zone") neighborhood and have their minds blown watching cowboys dancing arm-in-arm to ranchero music at Vaqueros Bar. Queer tourists wonder why they can't throw warehouse parties like the ones in Mexico City, where trans women, lesbians, gays, and everyone in between mingle together effortlessly. The city feels smart and cosmopolitan, and it has energy. There are pyramids. There are tacos. It's affordable. The list goes on.

Queer History:

"THE DANCE OF THE 41"

On November 17, 1901, a group of 41 men, about half of whom were dressed as women, mingled at a party in Mexico City. After police illegally raided the event, efforts were immediately made by the government to protect the names of those present, many of whom were members of the upper echelons of Mexican society. Soon after, rumors started to swirl about "The Dance of the 41." The attendees were subsequently identified and penalized in various ways, including public humiliation, jail time, and forced conscription into the army to carry out manual labor. Dressing as the opposite sex wasn't illegal, but the political climate of the era was charged, and so punishment was delivered.

This marked the first time that homosexuality was mentioned in the Mexican media, and for a country so deeply Catholic, the number 41 took on a particularly negative connotation. For years, 41 held the same bad luck energy as the number 13 does in many other cultures. These days, queers take pride in owning and flaunting the number 41, a subversion that underlines Mexico City's current status as a beacon of ultra-liberalism in an otherwise traditional country.

BY THE NUMBERS

1979
Year of the first gay pride event in Mexico City

2010
Year that same-sex adoptions became legal in CDMX

18
Number of states (out of a total of 32) in Mexico that allow gay marriage

2 1/2
Hours it takes to fly from gay-ass CDMX to gay-gay-gay-ass Puerto Vallarta, on the west coast of Mexico

Chat WITH A LOCAL

Sassy_Planet: Is the historic meaning of the number 41 something that you, as an average Mexican gay person, know about?

Paco: Yes. It was a dance with 41 people, all gays. There was drag. And [it's said that] the son-in-law of the president was there, so it was this huge thing.

Sassy_Planet: And then the number became bad luck in Mexican culture, but the gays reclaimed it?

Paco: Yes, and 2019 was also the 41st anniversary of the CDMX Pride parade. So for that reason it was a special year for us.

Zemmoa on Trans Visibility in Mexico City

Zemmoa, a trans artist, activist, and musician from CDMX, knows that Mexico City is a haven for queers worldwide—and she is proud to show visitors around. "People are always coming here," she says. "In the art and gay scenes, someone's always arriving in town. I'm constantly speaking English in Mexico."

Sassy Planet: Tell us a bit about yourself.

Zemmoa: I'm an artist in constant learning. I can be a singer and I can be a writer; I can be an actress and I can be a model and I can be an activist. I have so many ways to express myself. My music is the thing I love the most. When I was starting to do music I was almost the only trans person here doing that sort of thing. *RuPaul's Drag Race* wasn't the thing that it is now. It hadn't influenced Mexico. Now, it's a movement. A lot of things are happening after *RuPaul*.

SP: How do you think things have changed in Mexico City over time?

Z: When I was 18 there were queer people, but they were very high-up fashion people. There have been gay bars, like in Zona Rosa, since the 1980s, but the scene is bigger now. Over the years I've become closer to the trans community. I've found my niche. There are a lot of amazing trans women in CDMX who weren't here 10 years ago. Back then, it was just me. There are a lot of trans artists. I have trans musician friends, trans activist friends, trans YouTube beauty blogger friends. Everyone is improving our visibility. Things are growing. There's even a podcast from CDMX called *La Hora Trans* where you can find a lot of interviews with trans people, ranging from prostitutes to musicians like me.

SP: What parties do you go to?

Z: In CDMX there are new parties and clubs with weird fashion

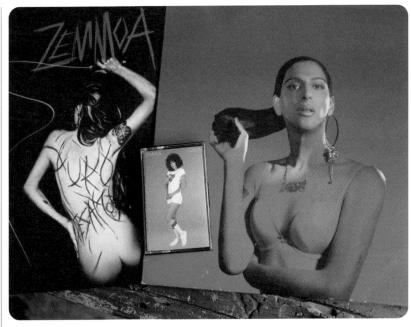

Zemmoa's records.

people and drag queens with all kinds of characters. For example, the party called Por Detroit has lots of queer, fashionable people. You have options: underground, hard techno, drugs, and more normal scenes like downtown or Zona Rosa. I have a friend that always says, "We are all trans." In a way, you change your body, you change your mouth, your eyes, your beard, your style. The best parties are always queer. Straight people know that, and they go. Suddenly it's a mix. It's always a mix.

SP: How would you describe Mexican people?

Z: We are very *one*. We're fun—we like to laugh a lot, we joke, we have a good sense of humor. We are friendly. We are warm. Family is very important for Mexican people. It's like we are all friends. If you smile at

someone on the street, they'll smile back.

SP: What more needs to be done for LGBTQ people in Mexico?

Z: The government is making changes step by step. Now, if you have HIV or if you're trans, you can go and get your medicine for free—someone is taking care of you. People still discriminate, but the government of CDMX isn't discriminating as much. You can get married in Mexico City.

With more trans artists and more people doing cool things, we can move things in the right direction. I feel excited and very inspired by the work of others. I don't feel alone anymore. I've found family. We are all, in a way, just trying to make a better Mexico.

Por Detroit:
Paying homage to the Detroit techno scene, this
dance party takes over unconventional spaces in
Mexico City and draws a fierce queer crowd.

Miami, Florida

There may be nothing original about including Miami, of all places, in a book about LGBTQ travel—it's been an international gay destination for decades, attracting over a million queer visitors each year. But the scene has transformed recently, with much of Miami's nightlife migrating 40 miles north to Fort Lauderdale.

The South Beach of *The Birdcage* may be a distant memory, but the city is still pretty queer. The exclusive gay spaces may have dwindled, but the White Party aesthetic of the 1990s has become mainstream. Gym-toned, surgically enhanced bodies—in or out of tight clothing—lounge in luxurious pool cabanas, in the bars of high-end Art Deco hotels, and on the sands of Miami's beaches.

While South Beach has vestiges of the circuit boy vibe, a truly creative queer scene has emerged just across the water on the mainland. Miami is home to some of the most cutting-edge, diverse, and unpredictable drag performers in the United

States. Shows happen almost every night of the week. Rock venue Kill Your Idols puts on shows every Monday, as well as drag queen-hosted karaoke, trivia, and bingo nights. On the third Sunday of every month, Corner, a small bar across the street from the city's most baller strip joints, turns into Counter Corner, an experimental drag revue featuring queens ranging from novice to legendary. Then there are the invite-only Lemon City Day School house music parties, which happen on select weekends in a private warehouse featuring a ball pit and a swing hanging below the neon lights.

In the recently developed arts district, Wynwood, a thriving alternative scene has become fertile ground for drag, with Wigwood, an annual showcase. The neighborhood even produces its own Pride weekend. On Thursdays, the backyard of hipster bar Gramps is turned over to DJ Hottpants for his Double Stubble party, which brings together emerging drag queens from all over South Florida.

Miami, from Basic to Exxxtra

Counter Corner

Double Stubble

Hotel Gaythering

Twist

Azucar

Palace Bar

Queer History:

THE LAST OF THE GAY BARS

A decade ago, you couldn't throw a rock in South Beach without accidentally gay-bashing someone at one of the city's 10,000 gay bars. Today, most of these venues have gone the way of the rollerblade. But two of the city's most iconic establishments have managed to survive the Great Fort Lauderdale Migration and continue to draw large crowds, gay and straight.

Palace Bar, with its pumping music and daytime drag shows a few steps away from the main gay beach, is a sidewalk spectacle. Its brunches have become the stuff of drag lore, with queens performing on the hoods of cars stuck in traffic and death dropping from the heights of double-decker tour buses.

A few blocks away sits the venerable Twist nightclub, which opened in 1993. The two-story complex on Washington Avenue—wrapped for some strange reason around a dentist's office—houses seven different spaces, each with its own unique music and vibe. Twist is a refreshing cross-section of gay life. In the back cabana, old-timers stuff cash into the G-strings of go-go boys gyrating to Lady Gaga. On the second floor, Latin couples expertly dance salsa to Caribbean rhythms.

(1)

(2)

1: DJ Hottpants cheers on the crowd at Double
Stubble. 2: Many drag shows at Double Stubble
feature collaborations between local performers
and dancers. 3: Queef Latina celebrates Counter
Corner's anniversary wearing a dress made of
the party's flyers. Next spread: Final performance
of the night at Counter Corner.

Montreal, Canada

Montreal's reputation as an open-minded "Sin City" dates back to as early as the age of American Prohibition. In the 1920s the city, which still sold alcohol legally and openly, turned into something of a party town for Americans aiming to get wasted. However, some might argue that its real spirit of freedom stems from an unlikely event: a moment of police brutality that targeted the local LGBTQ population.

On the morning of July 15, 1990, Montreal police surrounded the Sex Garage party venue, which occupied a loft space in Old Montreal, under weak pretenses that barely masked their true intentions: to target and punish partiers for nothing other than being queer. Police forced hundreds of people out of the space mid-party, with many prevented even from grabbing their belongings in the process, and proceeded first to verbally insult and then to physically assault them. The event traumatized, but then galvanized, the entire spectrum of queer life in the city, and Montreal's LGBTQ community responded by protesting like never before. Queer Montreal rapidly became organized, stronger, and fiercer, and in the 30 years since the Sex Garage raid the city has developed one of the most cohesive and proud queer communities in North America.

Florence Gagnon is Looking for the Ladies

Florence Gagnon is a native Québécoise who in 2014 started the event Où sont les femmes? ("Where are the Women?"), an intergenerational party for queer women in Montreal. She also founded Lez Spread the Word (LSTW), an LGBTQ+ organization and magazine devoted to producing content by and for queer women, among numerous other media projects.

Sassy Planet: What was it like coming out and moving to Montreal?
Florence Gagnon: It didn't go so well with my parents, so I left home earlier than expected. I moved to Montreal, 30 minutes away, with my girlfriend at the time. I've been living in Montreal since I was about 20, and I'm 32 now. Back then I was living in the Gay Village—it was still really vibrant then. It's been a problem, then and now, that the Village isn't really inclusive for everyone. It's mostly older white, cis gay men, but they've been working a lot to change it, and I've been a part of wanting to make this change.

SP: Are there other areas that you'd recommend checking out as a queer person? Do you not go to the Village at all as a local?
FG: There are so many other neighborhoods that are really LGBTQ-vibrant and active. Now I live in Mile-Ex. It's the more indie area. More lesbians, QTPOC, trans folks, queer-owned businesses; a bit more of an underground scene. The Village is still relevant for people coming from outside Montreal who don't know the local scene—they'll find a sense of belonging. If a visitor feels lost and wants to feel safe, the Village is great, but for many people who live in Montreal, Mile-Ex and the Plateau are more the scenes they would take part in. But we still all love to hang out in the Village during the summer. I also think the Village is important to older queers because there are a lot of non-profits and resources based there.

SP: What's been your contribution to Montreal's queer culture?
FG: In 2012 I created Lez Spread the Word. LSTW strives to defy prevailing stereotypes and provide a space for more positive models. At the beginning we were just a blog and were doing events, but it transformed into other projects along the way. We made a web series called *Féminin/Féminin* that was bought by Hulu and Amazon, and we created a magazine, *lstw*. I've also been involved in other

(1)

throughout the night, but they all come for different things. The crowd is really diverse. It's really the rendezvous of the month for queer women. For the past three years we've had guest DJs. Most of the time they're local celebrities of some sort, and they play for an hour.

SP: What about the weather situation—isn't Montreal in a state of constant frigidness and blizzardness for half the year? Does that affect the social scene?
FG: The weather doesn't prevent us from drinking and having fun. The biggest parties are during Pride season, but the biggest parties after Pride are in the winter. People go out less in winter, but when they do go out they have *fun*. If people decide to go out during a snowstorm, they'll go to a venue and they won't leave after two drinks—they'll stay till the end of the night.

SP: You make Montreal sound great to visit. What's it like to live there?
FG: It's a great place to live. It's cheap, and it's a big city but you don't feel the usual pressure of the city. Montreal is such a safe and calm place, such a vibrant city. It's really arts-oriented, and I think that's why people visit here, and why some end up staying.

organizations, like Pride at Work Canada, the Quebec LGBT Chamber of Commerce, and Pride Montreal. I think the scene has really evolved over the past 10 years. I've been more involved with things surrounding the arts. I think there are a lot of new things happening here.

SP: Impressive! What are some of the other neighborhoods in Montreal like?
FG: There's a lot of stuff going on outside the Village. There are a couple of spaces that are dedicated to queer stuff. Mile-Ex is like Brooklyn—there are tons of small pop-up spaces that are more LGBTQ-inclusive. Bar Le Ritz PDB is a venue for shows— they have big themed dance parties—and there are great spaces like Bar AlexandraPlatz. And Lez Spread the Word holds a monthly event called Où sont les femmes? It started as a lesbian night but more and more it's attended by bi, queer, pan,

nonbinary, and trans folks. We change venues every six to eight months. There's also Casa del Popolo in the Plateau. It's a venue for shows, but a lot of people from the community go there to have a drink.

SP: Can you tell us about Où sont les femmes?
FG: This party has always been different—it's not just an all-night dance party, and the crowd is a bit different. We always wanted to have the night be intergenerational. It's all ages. We start as an *apéro* (pre-dinner drink) event around 6pm, so we have a lot of power lesbians coming for a drink after work; and then it switches to the sort of cool crowd around 8pm; and then the younger lesbians come around 10pm. We have time to dance, to eat some food, have a drink, but the younger audience does the party from 10pm to 3am. So you can have 300 to 400 women coming

---

1: A *lstw* magazine event.
2: Montreal's Gay Village.
3: An Où sont les femmes? party.

(2)

(3)

Nashville, Tennessee

Turns out Dollywood and the state's somewhat phallic shape aren't the only gay things about Tennessee! Nashville, its capital, has an incredibly active and visible LGBTQ community that fits queerness into a Southern mold—and not the other way around. There's the obvious honky-tonk gay stuff geared toward tourists (gay bars are legally required to employ at least two Dolly Parton drag queens at all times in case one breaks a stiletto), but there's lots more to the city for those willing to ask around.

Despite this, Nashville is still in a very conservative state. In early 2020, for example, Tennessee became the latest state in the US to allow taxpayer-funded adoption and foster care agencies to discriminate against prospective

LGBTQ parents on religious or moral grounds. Luckily, Nashville is a shiny, sequined exception to Tennessee's traditionalism. The city's gayborhood, known as The District, extends along Church Street to the west of downtown. There's plenty of queer bar-hopping (and whiskey sampling) available to entertain visitors. But to experience the city like a true rhinestone cowboy—sorry, cow*person*!— a twirl through Nashville's bluegrass and country scene, one that includes more LGBTQ performers every year, is mandatory.

Christa Suppan's
Top Nashville To-Dos for Ho-Mos

"NashTrash bus tours are the best!"

"Wander the mom-and-pop shops in East Nashville."

"Check out the downtown scene— it's fun for a first- or second-timer."

"Grab a show at the Ryman Auditorium."

"And, of course, come to Lipstick for karaoke!"

Queer History:
LIPSTICK LOUNGE

Lipstick Lounge, a gay bar in downtown Nashville, opened its doors in 2002. "I came in as an owner a few months later," Christa Suppan explains. These days, the bar has a large lesbian fan base, but everyone is welcome. "Our tagline is 'a bar for humans,' and we mean that," she adds. The bar hosts trivia nights, a *Family Feud* parody show, and drag shows the first Friday of every month. However, what Lipstick Lounge is best known for is its karaoke, which is legendary. "It's really the best I've heard anywhere," Christa says.

(1)   (2)

Christa, who moved to Nashville from Illinois in 1993, thinks the city has made enormous strides toward acceptance of LGBTQ people in recent years. She describes it as a "bubble of acceptance" in an otherwise extremely conservative state. "It's quite lovely to be able to go to pretty much any bar and not feel like an absolute outcast," she says.

1: Christa Suppan and her partner.
2: Luscious red lips greet guests at Lipstick Lounge.

Chat WITH A LOCAL

Sassy_Planet: What's the LGBTQ scene like in Nashville?

Looking4: The scene in Nashville is big, but it's changing. Church Street had a lot of popularity 20 years ago but has started to change a lot recently.

Sassy_Planet: How so?

Looking4: Back then, it was basically just Church Street. There weren't many other places to go as a gay person. So you'd go to prime spots like Tribe for happy hour, followed by Play Dance Bar to catch the drag shows and dance.

Looking4: Canvas and Blue Jeans were down the street; that's where the less mainstream gays gathered. Then you have TRAX and Pecker's, which hold more of the grungy, leather, and older men. Lipstick Lounge has been around forever. It's the main lesbian bar.

Sassy_Planet: Are these places that people still go to?

A drag performance at Play Dance Bar.

Looking4: These places were iconic, and still are, but the buzz has dropped dramatically since Nashville has become more gay-friendly on the whole. Now there are super trendy places that are cool for everyone to go to, gay or straight.

Sassy_Planet: Oh yeah, like where?

Looking4: Brunch places! Everyone likes brunch.

New York City, New York

New York. The concrete labyrinth spread over islands, connected via subway tunnels, chronicled in countless films, books, and songs. All queers end up in this metropolis at some point—some to visit, others to stay. It's loud, it's expensive, it's dirty, and it's not for everyone. But it is, in many ways, the ideal place to visit. Walkable, gridded, and friendlier than you might expect, NYC's many gayborhoods cater to every conceivable niche.

The Best (Straight-Friendly) Things to Do in NYC

Literally everyone in New York is gay, so it can be super difficult to know where to take your one straight high-school friend when he comes to town—usually on, like, St. Patrick's Day—and wants to see the city. Fear not, young homo! We've racked our brains and have come up with this amazing list of options of very queer places where your hetero friends and family will feel SAFE.

Soul Summit in Fort Greene Park:
A free, old-school house music party held only a few times during the summer, with an incredibly racially diverse and queer/straight mixed crowd. Imagine getting sweaty in a park, during daylight, on a crowded makeshift dancefloor under the trees. Everyone's smiling ear to ear at this party.

MOOD RING in Bushwick:
Truly a bar for all types, this divey bar pays homage to the colorful world of Wong Kar-Wai films. It draws a younger crowd that doesn't ascribe to a single scene or category but that also isn't too cool to dance recklessly to DJs in the small backroom dancefloor.

Paradisco at Le Bain in Meatpacking:
A super gay daytime disco dance party that happens only in spring, on Sundays, on the rooftop of The Standard. Straight people might not like disco, but they do love sunsets on rooftops.

Happyfun Hideaway in Bushwick:
A mixed/queer DIY bar space started by the legendary Secret Project Robot art space crew, it doesn't get more Bushwick than this, in the best way possible.

Soul Summit.

(1)

Christopher Street Pier in the West Village:
Yes, it's that pier from *Paris is Burning*, but these days it's sort of fancy and covered in grass. Lie here on a blanket on a summer day and prepare to see a bunch of gays taking a stroll through, or plopping down with friends for a picnic or tanning session.

(2)

Julius' in the West Village:
One of the oldest gay bars in the United States, NYC gays cherish this landmark dive. Also, they serve amazing burgers. Yes, gay people eat food.

Ladyfag parties at locations asundry:
Ladyfag is a queer party personality, promoter, and fixture of NYC nightlife. Her epic, high-production-value parties happen throughout the year in Manhattan and Brooklyn, featuring her hand-picked selection of A-list DJs.

(3)

Pizza literally anywhere:
If you come to NYC and don't eat at least 40 slices of pizza, you're wasting your time. Artichoke is your most decadent buttery slice. L&B Spumoni Gardens in Brooklyn is your most controversial, bready slice. Joe's (all over the city) is your best standard slice. John's of Bleecker Street is an amazing coal oven slice. The list goes on and on and on.

Day trip to Sandy Hook Gunnison Nude Beach:
Take the ferry from Pier 11 in Manhattan to Sandy Hook in New Jersey, just under an hour away, and find yourself on a nude beach with a very significant gay zone (at its southernmost end). Check out hot guys, scrutinize their butts, and then squint to see Lower Manhattan in the distance.

1: Christopher Street Pier. 2: Performer Matty Crosland at Julius'. 3: Ladyfag's Battle Hymn party.

NYC's Reigning Disco Queen, DJ Lina Bradford

Lina Bradford, a New York City native, got her start performing and dancing in the queer bars of the East Village. She has since blossomed into a successful DJ, spinning her trademark collection of disco music (even before it was cool again) at bars and clubs across the US and Europe, including a legendary 10-year residency at Sip-n-Twirl in the Fire Island Pines.

Sassy Planet: Disco music has firmly taken hold of the queer scene in New York again, which is something you've helped to make happen—you've been spinning this stuff for 25 years now. Why do you think disco has become so popular again in NYC?

Lina Bradford: Yes honey, it's been my duty to school the children! I think it's a testament to the connection of being a storyteller and a DJ and putting out great music. It has everything to do with that. It's also a testament to our collective faggotry bone, honey, which connects us all to this type of music—it's not just pop rocks, honey, you've got some soul up in there. And the fact that these kids can come together and feel that for me, I live for it. Because you know I don't play commercial music—I don't know it, I don't listen to it, it just does not speak to me. I've never pimped myself out for coin to spin that type of music. So the fact that people still come correct and live for it—that's what I'm here doing.

SP: You DJed a super popular party in New York's Fire Island, at Sip-n-Twirl in the Pines, for 10 years straight. What was that like, and why did you stop?

LB: I know, who ever thought that a mixed Jewish girl would come and turn that island out four nights a week? There's only love there, great memories, but that's all over. I've always had an alarm clock in me for when it's time to go and do something—I've had that my whole life, from when I was performing, all that stuff. On my 10-year anniversary in the Pines, I said, I don't know what I'm going to do next, but it's just time for me to go. I've always left when I was at my peak. I can't ever go backwards. It would take away from that mystique and the magic of what that time there was.

Corey Craig: Pharmacist by Day, DJ by Night

Corey Craig has DJed everywhere, from Sydney's famed Mardi Gras celebrations to the Riviera Maya in Mexico. Though he saves countless souls on the dancefloor by night, by day he also saves actual lives—as a pharmacist at NewYork-Presbyterian Hospital. Not flying to Mexico or Mardi Gras anytime soon? You can also catch his house and disco tracks on his podcast, called, adorably, *COREYOGRAPHY*.

Sassy Planet: Tell us a bit about yourself.
Corey Craig: I moved to New York from Dallas in 2001, just before 9/11. When I'm not traveling and DJing, I'm also a pharmacist, so that sort of work keeps the other side of my brain occupied. I started DJing in NYC around 2006 and giving people mix CDs, and I ended up doing the Pride Pier dance in 2009 and sort of used that as a way to launch my career. Soon after that I started DJing Fire Island, Provincetown, Los Angeles, San Francisco, Sydney Mardi Gras, and eventually ended up producing my podcast, *COREYOGRAPHY*.

SP: What are your thoughts on the virtual disappearance of Chelsea, which was for a very long time NYC's main gay neighborhood?
CC: I think NYC is a victim of gentrification and the fact that, for so long, landlords could come along and raise the rent and then not worry about having tenants, and write off their losses. So now in Chelsea you have all these storefronts that never reopened, and that really took the allure of the neighborhood away.

Then you have people that move into Chelsea who don't know the LGBT history of the neighborhood, and they complain about the noise and the people in fetish gear at The Eagle. Our remaining gay spaces in Chelsea are surrounded by people who aren't friends of the neighborhood—as soon as the gay element shows itself, they have a problem. Every other block between 14th and 23rd Streets used to have a gay bar. Now it's just a handful, like Gym Sportsbar, REBAR, and The Eagle. It's a lot less than we used to have. The Eagle is an institution. It's a three-story place on the west side of town, and we need it. There's nothing else like it. I love the Sunday rooftop beer blasts there. I can't imagine NYC without that going on.

Brooklyn Is a Thing

Several years ago, fabulous gay people in Manhattan started to realize there was a mass of land across the East River, and it was called Brooklyn. Everyone seemed to be moving there, all the parties seemed to be happening there—there was even an HBO show centered around despicable twenty-something girls living their #bestlives set in the borough.

The story of the rise of Brooklyn is partially one of displacement, rapid luxury development, and rent hikes, but it's also a tale of resourcefulness and creativity on the fringes. For decades, gay venues in Manhattan (and worldwide, for that matter) seemed to be owned by a mob of disconnected, money-grubbing straight guys, cashing in on a captive audience of queers who relied on their LGBTQ-specific venues as a social lifeline. But gradually, Brooklyn queers, weirdos, and artsy allies started using the (slightly) more affordable real estate landscape across the river to their advantage. They opened nightclub and bar spaces that catered to their own communities, with a new set of rules, a focus on acceptance and tolerance, and a commitment to art-making.

Venues like Bossa Nova Civic Club, Happyfun Hideaway, Elsewhere, C'mon Everybody, Nowadays, and House of Yes have popped up across the borough within the last decade or so. Each is either queer-owned or queer-friendly and run by young, smart, seasoned nightlife figures with the goal of creating a more inclusive, less skeezy, less homogeneous, and more positive party experience for all.

What to Check Out in BK

There now exists a wide range of LGBTQ-specific parties for the many varied flavors of the queer spectrum that sell out all over Brooklyn's 70 square miles. Some of these nights, like Bubble T, The Carry Nation, Papi Juice, and Wrecked, have grown exponentially and gained international acclaim. Smaller venues draw queer crowds with specific musical styles and scenes, hosting parties such as Be Cute, Pat, Yalla!, Baby Tea, Dick Appointment, GHE20GOTH1K, Onegaishimasu, HARDER, Unter, and the afterhours party and space The Spectrum.

(2)

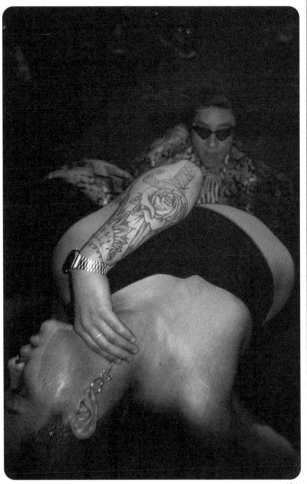

(1)

Also, be sure to get drinks at gay bars The Rosemont and Metropolitan and take advantage of their outdoor spaces—something else Manhattan doesn't have much of. And if iconic promoter Ladyfag is producing any parties the weekend you're in town, whether in Brooklyn or Manhattan, definitely check that out. The production value of her events is impressive, and the gays worship the ground she walks on.

1: Bubble T. 2—4: Papi Juice.

(3)

(4)

Omaha, Nebraska

GAY FREEDOM

newsletter of the
Omaha Gay Freedom League

O maha conjures up mental images of early aughts indie rock, billionaire Warren Buffett, and tumbleweeds. Queer-wise, it makes one think of Brandon Teena, the trans man brutally murdered south of the city in 1993 and whose story served as the basis for the movie *Boys Don't Cry*—not the most uplifting association. However, from the founding of the Omaha Gay Freedom League (which published its first newsletter, *Gay Freedom*, in 1972) to the very public and much-discussed transition of transgender college professor W. Meredith Bacon in 2005, Omaha has staked its own place in LGBTQ history.

These days, a visitor to Omaha will find a collection of standard Middle America gay club and bar offerings downtown. But a short drive to Benson, just a few miles to the northwest of the city center, magically transports you to what seems like a sprawling version of uber-cool Bushwick, Brooklyn.

"Uncontrolled Chaos" in the Benson District

Omaha native John-Paul Gurnett.

John-Paul Gurnett, a gay Omahan born and bred, co-founded Queer Nite—an LGBTQ party at a Benson-area bar called The Sydney—in early 2018. Queer Nite was created to provide an alternative to the overly white, heteronormative spaces elsewhere in the city. "People always say that Queer Nite reminds them of New York," John-Paul says. "I have to remind them that it's actually 100 percent Nebraska. What makes it feel like New York is that it's uninhibited. It's controlled chaos. We have a rotating lineup of DJs that each bring their own vibe. Crabrangucci serves trip-hop, Cayleen brings us bubblegum pop, and Desiring Machine broadcasts queer radio from the year 3000." Since the introduction of Queer Nite, The Sydney has transitioned from grimy goth-punk dive bar to grimy goth-punk (and now queer!) lounge.

Just down the block from The Sydney is the Petshop Gallery, which is run by a nonprofit organization called BFF (formerly Benson First Friday), of which John-Paul is also the director of communications. BFF, whose aim is to build community through arts engagement, initiated a Friday-night art crawl event in 2012 that has since grown and developed an LGBTQ and mixed following, bringing out the weirdos, artists,

A Queerniverse performance at MaMO.

and queers every week. BFF also includes in its programming MaMO, a 42-foot-long semi-trailer that has been converted into an alternative performance space, as well as Gen Q, an art program for queer youth involving a mentoring series and rural outreach initiative.

Of Omaha, and the Benson district in particular, John-Paul says, "There's a kindness here, and there are people doing cool things. We're figuring it out. It's very inclusive. Everyone is welcome to join. People coming through Omaha are really surprised by how nice people are. It's fun, and people here like to party." But then there's always the question: why tough it out in a smaller city—and in Omaha's case, a very Catholic city—in a super conservative state? "I believe in the idea of blooming where you are planted," John-Paul says. "I'd always dreamed of leaving Omaha for a larger city but resigned myself to the fact that that life wasn't for me. Omaha is often described as a 'nice place to settle'—a nice place to find a decent job and raise a family. That's not the life I wanted, so instead I just started creating the events and culture I wanted to see."

John-Paul Gurnett's
Top Omaha To-Dos for Ho-Mos

"Omaha's Henry Doorly Zoo, one of the best zoos in the world."

"Old Market, the cobblestone business district home to a variety of shops and restaurants."

"Hi-Fi House, a vinyl record library and museum."

"Fontenelle Forest, 26 miles of woodland trails and oak savanna."

"Runza. If California gets to have In-N-Out Burger, we get Runza. Tried-and-true Midwestern fast food."

BY THE NUMBERS

18,006
Roughly the number of LGBTQ people in Omaha

13
Minutes in a cab to get from the basic bars downtown to the alterna-queer spots in Benson

1
LGBT historical org: the Queer Omaha Archives at University of Nebraska Omaha

1
Number of anti-discrimination laws Nebraska supports out of 10 recommended laws listed by the Human Rights Campaign

Pittsburgh, Pennsylvania

The American version of the British TV show *Queer as Folk* made Pittsburgh seem like a gay Disneyland—and it kind of is. Locals are proud of their queer scene, which is larger than an outsider would assume based on Pittsburgh's size. The city's friendly, fun (but still edgy and punky) LGBTQ culture has earned it a reputation that extends well beyond western PA. Homespun parties like Honcho have become so popular they've started to travel to other regions. And the local dive bar Blue Moon has become the stuff of legend thanks to its role in sparking the careers of drag superstars Alaska Thunderfuck 5000 and Sharon Needles, among others.

Alaska Thunderfuck 5000's Nerves of Steel

Justin Andrew Honard, aka Alaska Thunderfuck 5000, needs no introduction. She's a household name for even the most casual fans of drag, having been the runner-up on the fifth season of *RuPaul's Drag Race* and the winner of the second season of *RuPaul's Drag Race All Stars*. Less known, though, are her humble drag roots.

She got her start at queer dive bars in Pittsburgh, where she was part of a ragtag group of punk queens (including fellow *Drag Race* winner Sharon Needles) who helped put the City of Steel's drag scene on the map. In addition to being a world-renowned drag superstar diva, Alaska has released three albums, titled *Anus*, *Poundcake*, and, most recently, *Vagina*.

Sassy Planet: Hiiiieeeyyy, Alaska! What's your connection to Pittsburgh?
Alaska: I grew up in Erie, which is two hours outside of Pittsburgh. So to me, growing up and coming out as a young queer person, Pittsburgh was the shining beacon, the city on a hill. It was the Land of Oz in the distance. So any chance I got, I went. I was the president of the art club in high school and demanded that we go to the Andy Warhol Museum and the

Mattress Factory museum for our yearly field trip. We would go to [the club] Pegasus, which allowed us to be under 21 and still go have a gay nightlife experience— I'll always remember that time.

SP: Does Pittsburgh have a big gay bar and club scene?
A: It has a ridiculous number of gay bars for a city of its size. The sheer amount is staggering. I think it has something to do

(1)

with the shit-ton of colleges in Pittsburgh that are stacked on top of each other. So I guess there's just a constant new influx of young people who want to go out and get wasted—and a lot of them are gay.

SP: How long did you live in Pittsburgh?
A: I went to the University of Pittsburgh, where I studied theater arts, and so I lived there for all four years of college. Then I went to LA for several years, and moved back to Pittsburgh for another four years while in a relationship.

SP: When did you start doing drag?
A: I first dabbled a little bit in college, but when I moved to LA I thought I'd put it behind me. I thought I wanted to be an actor, but then I realized there was no way I wanted to go on auditions to play straight people. I just wanted to be a crazy gay person, so I sort of fell into drag. It was my way of being sane and having fun, but then I started getting hired to do drag and went down that road. I'm still on that road, obviously—what else can I fucking do? Nothing.

SP: How did you get started in drag in Pittsburgh?
A: My very first drag show was at the Eagle, when [drag queen and porn director] Chi Chi LaRue came to town. She was giving out a $250 prize for the winner of a Fish Bowl contest, where you pick the song you're going to do out of a fishbowl, so you don't have any idea what you're going to perform. I picked "How Many Licks?" by Lil' Kim, to which I know every word. This was the Lord shining upon me. I won the night against the major drag queens of the city—you don't get paid $250 for a drag show, so everybody had come out. The second drag show I did was the Miss Pegasus pageant, where I got dog walked and came in dead last because I thought I was hot shit after winning with Chi Chi LaRue.

SP: Where would you recommend going if you want to see a good local drag show?

(2)

A: Blue Moon. It's where I really honed my drag. They had this tiny 4-by-4-foot stage and sound system that was held together by Scotch tape and chewing gum. That time was a really special moment of community. We were a bunch of freaky, weird drag queens, and our friends were in the queer punk scene, and they would come and watch our shows every week. Sharon Needles is my drag sister, and we were a couple at the time. So when she won *RuPaul's Drag Race* season four, and I was on the show the following year, I think all these queens started to think, "Oh, I need to work at the Blue Moon to be on *Drag Race* and be a successful drag queen." So it started out as a rough-and-

tumble misfit bar, but now all the drag queens are punching each other in the face to try to get a spot there. It's so unbelievable. I went to the Blue Moon just last year, and it's so incredible the queens they have there now—they make us look like a pile of crap!

SP: What else makes the city unique?
A: There's just something magical about it. Maybe it's the three rivers that converge, maybe it's the fucking 500 bridges the city has or whatever, but it's a special place. I'm from Western PA, so I'm completely biased, but I feel like there's a sort of frankness, honesty, and niceness that people from there have. The winters are

really, really hard; the summers are really, really hot—for the two months that summer lasts. I think we deal with that with self-deprecating humor. It's just sort of that vibe that's extremely welcoming, very authentic, and really feels like home to me. I hope it feels that way to people who visit, too.

1: Alaska onstage at Pgh Bro Club. 2: Alaska performs her song "Anus."

Pittsburgh's Queerest Bridges

Pittsburgh is home to almost 450 bridges, many of which identify as LGBTQ:

Alaska's
Top Pittsburgh
To-Dos for Ho-Mos

Go see a
Dixie Surewood show

"She has won major titles in drag, like Miss National
Comedy Queen, and reps at the Blue Moon."

Lucky's

"This place is downtown, and they have naked
strippers. Like, go-go dancers who are fully naked.
The great thing is they're not overly worked-out,
sculpted models like you'd see in West Hollywood.
They're just dudes."

Pgh Bro Club

"They do amazing parties. It's a really great
vibe, and they bring good people together—that's
really fun and sexy. It's fierce, and the music
is unbelievable."

The Mattress Factory

"This is a museum in an old mattress factory.
They give artists free rein to do whatever they
want with an entire floor or section of the
building. It's an amazing experience."

Documenting Queer Nightlife in PGH

Caldwell Linker has been documenting the queer scene in Pittsburgh for years. They've captured literally thousands of moments, from candid shots of LGBTQ parties to the rise of homegrown drag superstars Alaska Thunderfuck 5000 and Sharon Needles. "Having a vibrant queer scene in a town like Pittsburgh is work," Caldwell explains. "It's inviting folks you don't know well to things, publicizing the parties you want to see succeed, putting up with less-than-ideal venues at times, being the first person on the dancefloor, throwing the parties you wish someone else would throw, and showing up and not just complaining that there's nothing to do." This takes countless hours of behind-the-scenes work by DJs, performers, photographers, bar employees, owners, party organizers, and others. "But when it all comes together," Caldwell says, "it's glorious and intimate, and thrilling in ways that a scene in a bigger city never could be."

(2)

(1)

(3)

1 & 2: Late-night revelers at Pgh Bro Club.
3: Sappho, a benefit for Let's Get Free, a defense group for women and trans prisoners. 4: A house party. 5: A local LGBTQ protest.

(4)

(5)

Salt Lake City, Utah

Salt Lake City has a reputation for being backwoods, religious, and brimming with white Republican women named Kendra. However, outsiders are often surprised to find out just how queer the city is. It's had an openly gay mayor—something even New York has yet to accomplish—and is home to the seventh-largest LGBTQ population of any metropolitan area in the country. In 2018 the city council, which has three queer members, voted to name 20 entire blocks of Salt Lake after the early gay rights crusader Harvey Milk.

A lot of gays escape to Salt Lake from less accepting hometowns in neighboring states, making it a liberal haven in a conservative desert. Though better known for its skiing and rock climbing opportunities, it also has a vibrant queer nightlife scene with tons of clubs, bars, and parties to choose from on a weekly basis.

Utah, of course, is still predominantly Republican, and the socially conservative Mormon Church pervades pretty much every aspect of the state. But locals often credit this conservatism for helping the queer community push back harder against the dominant paradigm, creating a vibrant cultural and political scene in the process.

New City Movement

(1)

"The rooftop was going off, we had a basement lounge with hip-hop, and some live electronic producers were doing their thing," says DJ Jesse Walker. While he could be talking about the latest party at Elsewhere, Nowadays, or any number of other Brooklyn dance clubs named after an adverb, he's actually talking about an event he'd thrown the night before. "Everyone there was a former Mormon, of course."

Yes, an electronic music scene exists in "Molly Mormon" Salt Lake City, and the parties are probably more fun than where you live. But it wasn't always this way. In 1998, noticing a lack of good dance music and DJ culture, Jesse founded the nightlife collective New City Movement, "as a way to think abstractly about the future of nightlife and arts in Salt Lake City that didn't really exist at the time," he explains.

Jesse has been instrumental in putting the city's queer scene on the map. Originally from Idaho Falls, he moved to Salt Lake with his wife before coming out at the age of 24. Not long after that, he met his future husband, Mark Hofeling, and the two moved into a large warehouse in an industrial part of the city. "At first I was like, 'Are you crazy? This place isn't habitable,'" Jesse says. But Mark, who works as a film set designer, gave the building a major facelift—including a DJ booth with a sound system that rivaled any bar or club at the time.

The Warehouse, as it became known, quickly turned into a place for Jesse to test out his vision

(2)

1: DJ Jesse Walker, who founded New City Movement in 1998. 2: A New City Movement party in Salt Lake City.

(1)

of a revamped Salt Lake City nightlife scene. "For 10 years, it was like the Paradise Garage or Studio 54 of Salt Lake," he explains. "We broke all the rules. I think it helped open up everybody's minds to what could be possible in Salt Lake." Jesse soon began attracting well-known DJs to SLC—like Marques Wyatt, Mark Farina, and Doc Martin—putting Salt Lake's dance party scene on the map. "I was envisioning creating that 'new city' in the abstract, and just hoping it would become a reality someday," he says. "And it has come around, in a lot of ways."

Even hookup apps, which have "sup'd" and "into'd" queer nightlife into bloody oblivion in many other cities, haven't killed queer culture in Salt Lake. In some ways, Jesse says, the apps have even made the local nightlife better: "Back in the day, you literally had to go somewhere with your friends, get shitfaced, and put your beer goggles on to have sex," he says. "Now, people—in a really good way—go out specifically for the music and the community around it."

(2)

1 & 2: New City Movement's 20th anniversary party at Brick.

Jesse Walker's
Top SLC To-Dos
for Ho-Mos

Tinwell

"The patio at Tinwell in the summer. It's a great destination cocktail and dance club with a sweet tiki bar upstairs. Young, old, gay, straight, and everything in between roll through."

Gilgal Sculpture Garden

"A once-rotting pet project of a church stonemason turned public park, with insane sculptures."

Spiral Jetty

"Take a few hours to go see Robert Smithson's land art masterpiece *Spiral Jetty*, on the north shore of the Great Salt Lake."

Utah Pride

"Obviously. We have one of the biggest in the country and it's a joy to behold."

"Space Jesus"

"Visit the 'Space Jesus' statue at the visitors' center at Temple Square."

Chat WITH A LOCAL

Cliff: There used to be this really fun beach at the Great Salt Lake called Bare Bum Beach, but the police started raiding it in the 1990s, so I'm not sure if anyone still goes there.

Sassy_Planet: Oh, wow. Did you used to go?

Cliff: Yeah, it was fun in, like, the 1980s; a good place to cruise in the nude.

Sassy_Planet: Does anything like it still happen in Utah, or did the apps kill all that?

Cliff: Oh yes. Utah is actually really popular with nudists, gay and straight.

Sassy_Planet: Really?

Cliff: I mean … you do the math. In Utah, 80 percent of our population is crammed into less than 9 percent of the land mass. Everything else is basically a national park. It's just one giant beautiful outdoor playground. Lots to explore!

Sassy_Planet: But you can explore it with clothes on too, right?

Cliff: Yeah, but why would you?!

Queer History:
BARE BUM BEACH

In 1982, Deputy David Bishop, a sheriff with Utah's Juvenile Tactical Squad, saw a nude motorcyclist riding on a road near the Great Salt Lake. "I followed him and, lo and behold," the sheriff told *The Spectrum*, "Sodom and Gomorrah unfolded before my very eyes."

The strip of coastline, known as "Bare Bum Beach," had long been a popular spot for gays and nudists to cruise and sunbathe— and an easy place for police to rack up some citation money. In 1997, a sting operation against 31 men and three women, who were arrested at the beach, made local headlines. The group was cited for lewdness—punishable by up to six months in jail—and each person was given a $1,000 fine.

Though the beach isn't as active as it once was, thanks to police raids (and the distinctive smell of brine shrimp wafting from the nearby lake), locals say you can still spot a bare bum or two if you're lucky.

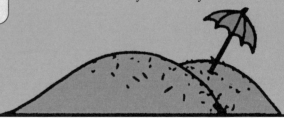

San Francisco, California

Many queers catch their first glimpse of San Francisco via an old Hitchcock film, or through reading one of Armistead Maupin's pioneering *Tales of the City* books. In media, the city comes off like a big, kooky village, filled with characters who reside in colorful wooden houses, existing freely and loving every moment of their California lives. In reality, San Francisco has become an expensive city, heavily influenced and changed by its local tech giants—but the queerness of the region has survived through efforts of resourcefulness and community. And while it may not be the pre-AIDS, 24/7 gay, mustachioed roller-disco paradise we all wish it still were, this fog-haloed metropolis is still filled with magic, especially if you look beyond the Castro.

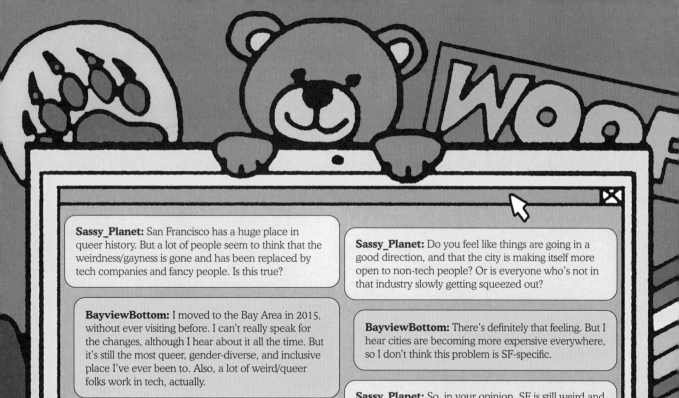

Sassy_Planet: San Francisco has a huge place in queer history. But a lot of people seem to think that the weirdness/gayness is gone and has been replaced by tech companies and fancy people. Is this true?

BayviewBottom: I moved to the Bay Area in 2015, without ever visiting before. I can't really speak for the changes, although I hear about it all the time. But it's still the most queer, gender-diverse, and inclusive place I've ever been to. Also, a lot of weird/queer folks work in tech, actually.

Sassy_Planet: Good to know. Is it hard for younger, less wealthy queers to move to SF since it's so expensive, or is there still housing available if you maybe have friends and connections who can hook you up?

BayviewBottom: Yes to both. I live with a daddy bear guy I met at Lazy Bear Weekend who offered me a room in his house for cheap, otherwise idk if I'd be able to afford it here. But people are still figuring out ways to do it. And I think it's still cheaper than NYC, since the spaces here are generally larger. You can also get good deals in the East Bay.

Sassy_Planet: Do you feel like things are going in a good direction, and that the city is making itself more open to non-tech people? Or is everyone who's not in that industry slowly getting squeezed out?

BayviewBottom: There's definitely that feeling. But I hear cities are becoming more expensive everywhere, so I don't think this problem is SF-specific.

Sassy_Planet: So, in your opinion, SF is still weird and queer, and you can live there if you're not a billionaire?

BayviewBottom: Yeah, it can totally be done. Lots of people have a little side hustle, whether it's working the door at a bar, throwing a party, walking dogs, selling drugs. It's doable. I also have to mention that the community here is strong and loud and takes care of the queerdos. Juanita More (a local legendary drag queen) runs a FB apartment listing for queers, and all three of the jobs I've gotten here were through my queer friends. So it's not all ruthless. If you're a loving person, people will want you around and help you out. This city can definitely spit people out if she's not feeling them, though.

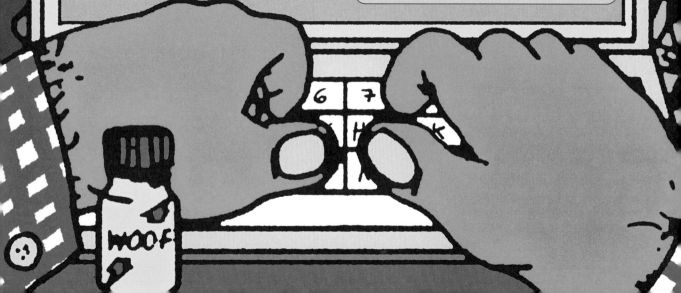

Oscar Pineda and His Collective of Studs

Oscar Pineda is one of 17 people who collectively own and oversee the legendary San Francisco gay bar the Stud. The bar first opened in 1966 and took up residence at 399 9th Street beginning in 1987. Although the Stud lost its home in 2020, Pineda assures us that the iconic LGBTQ venue will continue, in some form, as one of the country's longest-running queer bars.

Sassy Planet: How did you end up living in San Francisco?
Oscar Pineda: I moved to San Francisco in 2008, kind of on a whim. I was living in Portland, Oregon, at the time. I came down for [BDSM and leather event] Folsom Street Fair, and on my way to the train station to go home, I got sort of a sinking feeling and felt really sad to leave. Growing up Latino in Portland, it was kind of rough— I wouldn't say I felt like an outsider there, but coming here to San Francisco, on my first day I was welcomed with open arms by a bunch of Latino kids I'm still friends with to this day.

SP: Is San Francisco still lovable?
OP: Yes. There's still a lot to fall in love with here. The city has changed, and I've gone through

my moments where I'm kind of over it, but there's always something happening, whether it's Pride, or a protest, or the way the community comes together—those are all reasons why I'm still here. That's one thing that hasn't changed. The queer party scene is really tight here. It's full of love and acceptance. To me, that's the most beautiful thing about San Francisco.

SP: What's it like being part of the Stud collective?
OP: There was a guy named Michael who owned the Stud. The owner of the building sold it to a new owner, and the rent on the Stud was going to go super high. Michael was like, "I'm not going to deal with this anymore, I'm going to let it close." So a collective was formed to take over the space. I wasn't one of the original people, but I was invited into the collective later

(2)

(1)

on. People were asked to put down money so we could buy the liquor license from Michael, and we extended our lease for two years, knowing we'd eventually have to move to a new location. The rent went up over those two years and none of us was making any money; it was just a labor of love to try and keep the space open. The space unfortunately had to close, and we don't know when we'll open again as a club. We decided to let that building go and start to make plans for a new space. We all got into this because we wanted to save the place.

The Stud is the place where I met a large group of my friends. It has that sentimental value for me. As far as the history goes, it was always a place in a male-

dominated club scene that was welcoming toward women, drag queens, trans folks, and people of color. The Stud originally opened in 1966, and this last location we had was its second location. We just really want to keep it going. It's important to a lot of people. I don't know what the next version of the space will look like yet.

SP: What's it like going out and throwing parties in SF?
OP: The thing about SF is there's not a ton of options for things to do all the time. You sort of have to be plugged in. For the people here that are doing things,

1: The Stud. 2: Creme Fatale performs at Vivvy's Grand Opening at the Stud.

making things happen, it's a labor of love—a lot of times we aren't making money on these parties we throw. It's hard here because there are a lot of restrictive laws regarding liquor and when venues have to close, but we find a way to make it happen. There are a lot of fun daytime parties here, and that's one way we work around some of those restrictions.

SP: How can visitors find out what parties are happening on a given night?
OP: Just make friends when you get here. Whoever you meet might know what's up. Tourists sometimes expect our parties to be like NYC, and we aren't like that. San Francisco operates like a small town.

SP: What are the queers like in San Francisco?
OP: The vibe here is California, it's West Coast. It's almost silly, sort of. People are having fun and not taking themselves too seriously—with fashion, with everything. A San Francisco dancefloor is high energy, and everyone's got a big smile on their face. People get messy, but everyone just takes care of each other. We all have our fun, but we do it responsibly and look out for one another.

(1)

1: Tirell Cherry on the go-go box at the Stud. 2: The dance-floor warming up for PRISSY.

(2)

Oscar Pineda's
Top San Francisco To-Dos for Ho-Mos

Marshall Beach

"Gay nude beach near the Golden Gate Bridge."

The Botanical Garden

"Located in Golden Gate Park."

Take a hike

"Walk through Chinatown up to Grace Cathedral, and then over to Coit Tower."

Mexican food

"Have a burrito at La Taqueria. Order it *dorado*, meaning golden or crispy."

Dolores Park

"Everyone hangs out there, drinking, being happy, with a beautiful view of the city."

Seattle, Washington

Historically, Seattle's gay area was concentrated in the Capitol Hill neighborhood—and it still is—but as the local LGBTQ community has grown, so too have the number of smaller gayborhoods around the metropolis. The city is among the most progressive in the country and has long been friendly to queers: LGBTQ workers have been protected here since 1973. Of course, Seattle must take responsibility for unleashing the unrelenting heterosexuality of Foo Fighters onto the world. But all is forgiven thanks to the plentitude of queer icons who live here, including actor and musician Carrie Brownstein, sexpert Dan Savage, and *RuPaul's Drag Race* winner Jinkx Monsoon.

Matt Baume, Seattle's Queer Media Historiographer

Matt Baume, a self-described "writer, podcaster, and weirdo," is also Seattle's foremost Queer King of the Internet. He produces the podcast *Sewers of Paris*, in which he interviews LGBTQ people about the entertainment media that's influenced their lives; a YouTube series called *Culture Cruise*, about LGBTQ milestones in film and TV; and *Queens of Adventure*, a comedy podcast that involves (what else?) drag queens playing *Dungeons & Dragons*.

Sassy Planet: Can you describe Seattle and explain how it's changing, from your own, queer perspective?

Matt Baume: I'm originally from Connecticut, and I've lived in Seattle for six years. I think Seattle's done better than other cities in certain ways—we've been able to build housing better than cities like San Francisco and maintain slightly more affordable rent. Queer culture is going to change no matter what. I do think Seattle fosters many great queer communities. I live in Capitol Hill, which used to be the cheaper place that queers came to. It was gritty and scrappy, and now there's lots of construction and things are shiny and bright, and a lot of queers have moved away to outlying areas. I've noticed the community has dispersed a lot

in the past few years. There are little mini gayborhoods around the city that are getting stronger. As much as tech money has displaced queers on Capitol Hill, technology sort of allows these communities to stay in touch and foster their own communities wherever they wind up.

(1)

SP: When people think about Seattle, they think about grunge and Starbucks and tech companies like Amazon. Why would you say it's worth visiting as an LGBTQ person?

MB: Seattle is the most beautiful and most generous city I've ever lived in. It's got this incredible physical beauty, with the mountains and the forest and the beaches. The personality of the city is one of real kindness and compassion. When I moved here I noticed people waving each other through intersections or bussing their

own trays at restaurants. People here volunteer and show the neighborliness of a small town, but with the sophistication of a larger city.

SP: Tell us about the queer projects you produce.

MB: I've got so many weird little projects. I make *Sewers of Paris*, a podcast where I talk to queers about the entertainment that's influenced their lives. I make *Culture Cruise*, which is a YouTube series about LGBTQ milestones in entertainment, TV, and film that provides historical context. I make *Queens of Adventure* with my partner James Morris, a comedy podcast and live show that involves drag queens playing *Dungeons & Dragons*. We have our core Seattle cast for the podcast, but we also do live shows in other American cities. And I take nightlife photos, as well as writing about Seattle queer news for the city's weekly publication *The Stranger*. So what I do is really a mix of different ways of showing people what's going on in their world and who's in their world. When I take nightlife photos, I get to see familiar faces and create images of this beautiful queer life we get to lead. We're so fortunate that we get to be queer and have fun in ways that are sort of magical. I love capturing that and showing people how great it is to be gay.

SP: What's your favorite queer space in Seattle?

MB: The best gay bar on the West Coast, in my opinion, is Pony. It's this weird bar on this weird

(2)

triangular plot of land. It was a gas station and then a florist's shop, and then it was a shack for a while that was going to get torn down, but the owners were able to put in this gay bar there temporarily. The economy didn't perform as well as expected, and so the bar was allowed to stay for the long term. It's been there about a decade now. It's this

(3)

(4)

tiny little messy building, which means that it can constantly change and shift and adapt. There's always strange art going up or some weird night going on. It's small, so if you have 20 people in there, the night is a success. There's also a beautiful patio with a great view of the surrounding neighborhood.

SP: Give us a juicy nugget from Seattle queerstory.
MB: My favorite story is about this gay bar from the 1970s called Shelly's Leg. The story behind it is that it was Bastille Day and there was some sort of parade, and there were these confetti cannons. One of them got really wet and it ended up shooting this huge wet wad of confetti into a woman named Shelly, and it injured her and she ended up losing her leg in this incident. But with the payout she got from her lawsuit, she opened a bar called Shelly's Leg. It was the first disco in Seattle, and I think it was the first openly gay gay bar. It was 1973. So it really changed the culture in terms of things being open and out in the city—Seattle didn't have gay civil unrest in the way many other cities did, like Stonewall in New York or Compton's Cafeteria in San Francisco, so this bar really changed things. Shelly's Leg didn't last very long, though. I think it was open for around four years, and then a tanker truck full of gasoline crashed into it and basically blew it up (I don't think anyone was injured). It was an over-the-top existence from start to finish. I guess I love how *incendiary* the whole thing was.

1: Capitol Hill. 2 & 3: *Queens of Adventure* live shows.
4 & next spread: Pony.

Matt Baume's
Top Seattle To-Dos for Ho-Mos

See a Betty Wetter show

"She's a fantastic Seattle drag queen."

Vashon Island

"Take a ferry there for a small-town hippie experience. It's a cute, sweet day trip. There are a lot of queer farmers out there. Tiny little shops in a really adorable Pacific Northwest town."

Raygun

"For video games and board games—a great nerdy, fun place."

Sexy arts fests

"Visit during the Seattle Erotic Art Festival to see amazing, creative, innovative stuff. Or come during HUMP!, the amateur porn film festival curated by Dan Savage. It's a very ephemeral experience—people make and screen films, and then they're all destroyed at the end."

Pony

"The best gay bar."

South

Bogotá, Colombia

When it comes to LGBTQ liberation, Colombia is among the most advanced regions in Latin America—and not just because Shakira, the country's homegrown pop diva, was the first to speak up for the rights of queer canines everywhere with her gay pup anthem "She Wolf." The country passed comprehensive anti-discrimination laws in 2011, legalized same-sex marriage in 2016, and in 2019 Bogotá became the first capital city in the western hemisphere to elect a lesbian mayor. Bogotá is also home to what is thought to be the biggest queer club in Latin America. Theatron de Película, housed in an old theatre, has five floors and 13 rooms and can hold up to 8,000 people an evening—*muchísimo queers!* Locals will be quick to point out the less "mega" aspects of queer Bogotá as well, like the gay-friendly salsatecas, intimate dive bars, and queer-owned businesses.

Papi Boys

Modeling a Papi Boys shirt.

With clothing items named things like Starboy Diary and Oh My Twink!, apparel brand Papi Boys makes no secret of the clientele it's courting: hairy bears.

    … Kidding! These clothes are made for Timothée Chalamet and pretty much no one else. The boys behind the brand have dipped their toes into a different arena as well: nightlife. Several years back, they opened Sauna—which was *not* a sauna (there are plenty of those elsewhere in Bogotá) but a popular gay bar that served as something of an alternative to the megaclub Theatron de Película. Unfortunately, the bar closed in May 2019, but the spirit continues in the Papi Boys brand.

Chat WITH A LOCAL

Sassy_Planet: What's queer about Bogotá?

Busco: Everyone will tell you to go to Theatron, and you should. It's where everyone goes—a megaclub with a mixed crowd.

Sassy_Planet: What's the gay scene like more generally in Bogotá?

Busco: It's been easy for me to be openly gay here. It's really accepting. But Colombia has many contrasts. In general, Bogotá is a good place for an alternative way of life, although homophobia is still present in everyday life. You could maybe walk hand in hand with your boyfriend in a neighborhood like Chapinero or an upper-class area, but it's uncommon behavior still.

Sassy_Planet: How would straight people react in one of the less accepting areas?

Busco: They probably wouldn't do anything. And it's funny because a lot of the gay clubs have become really popular and trendy. Straight people like to mingle with us now in nightlife.

Sassy_Planet: Is there more underground gay stuff too?

Busco: Yes, there are lots of strip clubs and saunas and darkroom parties, things like that. Places like Manbar, where you can go and drink and play around with other guys. If you need a reference, think of Lab.Oratory in Berlin—it's like that.

Sassy_Planet: Any good lesbian bars?

Busco: There's a lesbian bar called Moza. It's kind of like the Cubbyhole in New York.

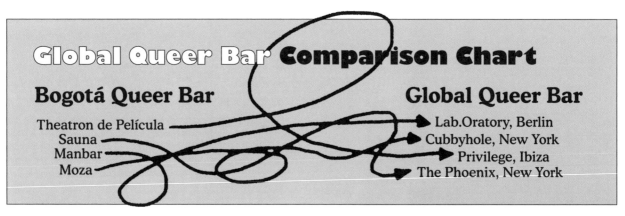

Global Queer Bar Comparison Chart

Bogotá Queer Bar

Theatron de Película
Sauna
Manbar
Moza

Global Queer Bar

Lab.Oratory, Berlin
Cubbyhole, New York
Privilege, Ibiza
The Phoenix, New York

Chat WITH A LOCAL

Sassy_Planet: What's the scene like for queer women in Bogotá?

Catalina: There are some lesbian-only parties, but they're not all the time. All the clubs and gay-friendly places gather straight and gay people; it's not just for girls or guys like it used to be, when there were lots of parties just for girls, no boys allowed. It has changed a lot. Owners of clubs are more open to including more LGBT people—so you can go to a straight bar and see a lot of gays, or drag queens doing their shows. People really like that. Like, there's a bar called Kaputt and it's gay-friendly. At all the places my friends and I go, if my friend is kissing her girlfriend, it's fine.

Sassy_Planet: So the city is pretty LGBTQ-friendly on the whole?

Catalina: Yes, it's open and friendly. I've never been in a position of discrimination or anything like that. Though I also think it's easier for women, and for me, because I don't dress or look like a butch lesbian.

Sassy_Planet: There's a gay salsa scene in Bogotá. What's that like?

Catalina: Yes! I love to dance. I sometimes go to Vintrash bar. They play crossover, like vallenato, salsa, and merengue. There was a gay bar I really liked, El Mozo, but they closed last year. They still do parties, but in other places now. The only gay bar around is Theatron. But I prefer to go to gay-friendly bars.

A peformance at Theatron de Película.

Sassy_Planet: Why do you think everything else closed down?

Catalina: Everybody now is so open-minded; times have changed. People don't like to go just to gay bars. All these clubs are gay-friendly and open-minded, so everybody goes. Gay people don't just want to be around gay people.

Sassy_Planet: How has the LGBTQ scene in Bogotá changed since you were younger?

Catalina: It has definitely changed a lot. Now, people are more open to going out and having fun without fear. They can dress and act like they want without judgment. People who are gay are considered normal. People are getting used to seeing two guys walking hand in hand, or girls dressing like boys. Of course, there are some who don't support LGBTQ people, but more people are realizing that love is love and just let people be how they are.

Catalina's
Top Bogotá To-Dos
for Ho-Mos

Video Club

"Go here for a fun night out."

Chapinero

"For amazing food experiences in all the great restaurants, visit this neighborhood in the north of the city."

El Centro

"Take a walk downtown for nice views."

El Mercado de Las Pulgas

"Visit this flea market to buy second-hand items as well as jewelry, clothing, and accessories made by locals."

Buenos Aires, Argentina

Buenos Aires has one of the most visible, developed LGBTQ scenes in all of South America. Queer life here spreads out across the city, with a particular concentration in *barrios* like Palermo, San Telmo, and Recoleta. The region's gay nightlife is vibrant, weird, and doesn't get going until very, very late. If you show up to the club any time before 3am, just know you'll be tangoing solo until the party starts.

Performance Artist Agustín Ceretti Wants to Serenade You in Bed

Agustín Ceretti, a performer and artist based in Buenos Aires, is known for his crazy shows that involve stuff like singing in his underwear in a bed. He also works as a designer for clothing brands, publishers, musicians, parties, and exhibitions, and is a resident artist at UV Estudios, a gallery combining visual art and sculpture with movement and performance. He performs across Buenos Aires and South America and is signed to the record label Ostras Formas.

Sassy Planet: Describe your work for us.
Agustín Ceretti: I'm an artist and graphic designer and also an underground pop star. As an artist I work with big objects and sculpture as well as performances, shows, and concerts. In my shows, I use objects and sculptures as stage design. I'm part of UV, a Buenos Aires gallery and artistic project.

SP: What are the queer art, music, and nightlife scenes like in Buenos Aires? And how are they different from other cities in South America?
AC: Buenos Aires is full of gays. There are a lot of gay and queer artists, musicians, and DJs in the city, and of course they're all underground. I don't know

if other places in South America are the same, but in Buenos Aires much of the queer scene happens in different art spaces. Obviously, there are also a lot of nightclubs and parties, but in recent years especially, new galleries have become important spaces where artists can develop ideas and aesthetics. Here's a few [good local] musicians: Dani Umpi, Matt Montero, Keity Moon, Aldo Benítez, Kobra Kei, Ibiza Pareo, Ignacio Herbojo, and Daiana Rose.

SP: Tell us about the UV art collective that you're part of.
AC: UV was started in 2015 and is directed by Violeta Mansilla. It's made up of nine different artist projects: Básica TV, Lolo y Lauti, Maruki Nowacki, Emilio Bianchic, Rodry & Lenny, Lulo Demarco, Guzmán Paz, Hoco Huoc, and me. All of us have

a great sense of humor and taste. We also love to throw big parties at every opening. We really love music and partying.

SP: What are your shows like?
AC: My shows are highly energetic—like a really mainstream pop artist with no budget. I like to make my own scenery and try to tell a little story in every show. I don't have musicians onstage; just me, myself, and a mic. The songs are pop, fun, and everybody's dancing and screaming.

SP: What's it like to be gay in BA?
AC: Buenos Aires is an excellent city for being gay. We have gay bars just like the rest of the world, and really big, mainstream gay clubs. And there's a really big scene for underground parties. Most of them are raves.

Agustín Ceretti performs.

Queer History:
TANGO QUEER

Every week Buenos Ayres Club, a salsa club in the San Telmo neighborhood of Buenos Aires, holds a queer tango night hosted by a group called—appropriately enough—Tango Queer. The group was started in 2007 by a woman named Mariana Docampo as a place for LGBTQ tango enthusiasts to dance without judgment. Her night has become incredibly popular in the years since, and even spawned the seven-day International Tango Queer Festival, which includes a number of workshops, events, and performances focused on LGBTQ tango.

Agustín Ceretti's
Top Buenos Aires To-Dos for Ho-Mos

Buy a ticket to any *teatro de revista*

"These are like music and comedy sketch shows with dancers and lots of feathers. There are a lot of theaters on Calle Corrientes that offer this kind of show."

Check out the parties

"For parties, you must go to Dengue Dancing at Gong Disco. It's an original club from the 1960s in the center of the city and has great music. And Amix, for the best pop music party ever! La Jolie is a classic gay club held on Wednesdays, and it's free. Fa Got Party is a leather rave. Vicio y Perversión is an extreme queer and kind of fun sex party, and Los Fiesteros is a sex club."

Shop at a fun boutique

"Visit Concha Espacio to get awesome looks to tour the city in."

See some art

"La Botica del Ángel and Fundación Klemm are the gayest art spaces. You must go!"

Salvador, Brazil

With a population of over 3 million people, Salvador, Brazil's third-largest city, boasts plenty to keep a queer busy for a week or two. Dozens of gay bars, clubs, and saunas line Rua Carlos Gomes, a mile-long stretch that's home to the heart of the region's queer scene. The coastal city also has tons of gay beaches—including Porto da Barra, Todos os Santos, and Praia dos Artistas. What may be more surprising to visitors, however, is that Salvador is the city many LGBTQ Brazilians flock to each year for Carnival instead of the more globally famous celebrations in Rio de Janeiro.

Chat WITH A LOCAL

Sassy_Planet: We heard that Carnival in Salvador is more fun for the gays than the one in Rio. Is this true?

PortoCarmona: Depends on who you ask! Both are fun, but they're really different.

Sassy_Planet: How so?

PortoCarmona: Carnival in Rio is more popular with gay tourists. A lot of Brazilians come here to Salvador instead. Carnival here is a bit less … polite.

Sassy_Planet: Less polite? In, like, a good way?

PortoCarmona: Yes! But it depends on how comfortable you are. Brazilians have less of a concept of private, personal space than Americans or Europeans do, so foreigners are often surprised by how aggressive the gay scene is in Salvador. If you go to a party and walk through a crowd, you might end up kissing two, three, or ten people before you get to where you're trying to go.

Sassy_Planet: What if you're not interested in kissing someone?

PortoCarmona: You just push them away a bit and shake your head. They'll understand and will stop. Still, you should go with friends, not alone, and never bring your cell phone to Carnival because you'll lose it.

Sassy_Planet: But … what about Instagram?!

PortoCarmona: Lol. Don't risk it! The scene is crazy in Rio too, but there are many more tourists there, so it's a bit more polite. Also, the music is very different. In Salvador, we're mostly Black and have Afro-Colombian music and drummers; in Rio, the music is more electronic.

Sassy_Planet: Is there anything you'd say is better about Rio's Carnival?

PortoCarmona: In Salvador, you have to buy a ticket and they give you a shirt you have to wear the whole time. Not everyone can afford it. Also, because you have to wear the shirt, the costumes are less over the top and fun than in Rio. For foreigners, Rio is more the Carnival you think of.

Sassy_Planet: Anything else that makes Salvador's Carnival unique?

PortoCarmona: Daniela Mercury! She's amazing— a lesbian singer from Salvador. If she's performing, you have to see her.

Queer History:
DANIELA MERCURY

In 2013, one of Brazil's most famous singers, Daniela Mercury—who has sold over 20 million records worldwide—made waves in Brazil (and abroad) when she divorced her husband and came out as a lesbian, marrying Malu Verçosa, a journalist, later the same year. Born in Salvador in 1965, Daniela got her start singing in the city's local bars. Long known as an outspoken voice for Brazilian women, she quickly took up the mantle of fighting for LGBTQ  equality in her music as well. In 2015 she again caused a stir with her album *Vinil Virtual*, whose cover features a nude Daniela wrapped around her wife, *à la* John Lennon and Yoko Ono.

Santiago, Chile

Queers in Santiago, Chile, were violently targeted during the oppressive years of Augusto Pinochet's dictatorship, which lasted from 1973 to 1990. But in the decades since, the LGBTQ scene here has flourished. The main gay area in the city is Bellavista, which is located between the Mapocho river and San Cristóbal Hill and includes most of the queer bars and clubs. The city is also home to the historic Fausto Discotheque, which opened in 1973, survived the Pinochet years, and claims to be the oldest continually running gay club in all of South America.

Chat WITH A LOCAL

Sassy_Planet: Is Chile a queer-friendly place in general?

Felipe: It depends. I'll say that right now it's pretty friendly in the places tourists usually go. It's a conservative country, but it has opened up to the LGBT community a lot in the last few years. It's a safe place to visit. It's not Russia. The last five years have been really great for the empowerment and respect of the LGBT community. Now there's a legal form of civil union between queers. It's not marriage, but still.

Sassy_Planet: What are the best gay places and things to do?

Felipe: There's a Líder supermarket branch that's almost only gay people cruising, on Monjitas Street in the Bellas Artes district. It's funny to go there—it's like Grindr with groceries. There's also Fausto, which is a disco for bear-ish gays. They have a drag show called Amigas y Rivales, which had its own YouTube reality show too.

Fausto Discotheque, the longest-running gay bar in South America.

Felipe's Top Santiago To-Dos for Ho-Mos

"Santiago Metropolitan Park—it's huge, and set on a hill in the middle of the city. It has parkland, the National Zoo and a Japanese garden at the bottom, and two swimming pools on top. And you can look out over the city."

"The Lastarria/Bellas Artes area— it's the cultural and gay 'hood."

"Persa Bio Bío is an absolutely huge flea market. A cool way to spend a Sunday morning."

"Centro Cultural Palacio de la Moneda. This is a really good cultural center beneath La Moneda (the presidential palace), with great exhibitions. The Cineteca Nacional is there too, so there are always movies playing. The Blue Jar, a restaurant and coffee place I really like, is nearby."

"La Vega Central, Mercado Central, and Mercado Tirso de Molina: the fruit market, the fish market, and the market in between. Visit for the chaos and smells, for groceries, or cheap restaurants serving classic Chilean dishes."

São Paulo, Brazil

W hen foreign queers imagine the gay scene in Brazil (as we all frequently do), images of bronzed, banana-hammocked boys frolicking together on Rio de Janeiro's beaches naturally come to mind. For local *brasileiros*, though, the heart of the country's scene is over 250 miles to the west of Ipanema, in São Paulo. Rio, we're told, is not the nation's gay capital any

other time of year except Carnival—and even that is a hotly debated topic among queer locals. (If you have an hour or ten to spare, ask a group of Brazilian gays which city hosts the better Carnival: Rio or Salvador.) Besides those few days in February, São Paulo is the undisputed queen of the queers.

Samba Zine, São Paulo's Black Queer Magazine

Several years ago, Juliano Corbetta, the editor in chief of *Made in Brazil* (a well-known men's fashion magazine based in São Paulo), started shopping around an idea to advertisers. He wanted to make an issue completely dedicated to the Black models and artists in the state of Bahia, an area of the country rich in Afro-Brazilian history and culture.

(1)

"No one wanted to sponsor a magazine that was going to be all Black boys," Juliano says. That experience, paired with the presidential election of Jair Bolsonaro in 2018—who has a history of engaging in casual hate speech against Black and queer people—made Juliano realize the project was actually more important than ever, despite the lack of funding. So he decided to create an entirely new magazine, called Samba Zine, that would push his concept even further. In addition to exclusively featuring Black models, the mag would use Black photographers, stylists, and writers. "We wanted to make it not only focused on Black artists, but super queer, focused on artists that are moving the culture forward," he explains.

To make a truly comprehensive project focused on young Black queer people, he also decided to partner with local apparel brand Fiever. Together, they channeled proceeds from certain

items to an organization in São Paulo called Casa 1, which provides housing for queer homeless youth. "With this project we were really trying to take some responsibility for the political moment in Brazil, and I'm happy with the way it came out," Juliano explains, adding that he hopes to continue publishing *Samba Zine* on a biannual basis.

(2)

1: Juliano Corbetta. 2: Cover of the first issue of *Samba Zine*.

(1)

(2)

(3)

(4)

1-4: Spreads from the first issue
of *Samba Zine*.

(1)

1 & 2: Images from the magazine's first issue.
Next spread: Artist Samuel de Saboia in
Samba Zine.

(2)

Juliano Corbetta's Top Queer Dance Parties in São Paulo

Dando:
"Dando started out at a smaller venue, with a darkroom where people get naked and have sex. It was also very Berlin, in a way, in terms of the music. But then it became super popular and now it's in these big warehouse spaces. The music is mostly electronic. It's a new scene for São Paulo, but I grew up with this while living in New York—back in the late 1990s and early 2000s, every club there had a darkroom. But for the younger generation here, the idea of people going to a party and meeting someone in person and not on Grindr is new. They're not used to physical contact when going out."

Mamba Negra:
"This party is like Berghain in Berlin in terms of ambience. But it has sort of become a space for young Brazilian DJs and drag performers, too, and the party goes on for hours. There's this amazing trans DJ, Valentina Luz, who's kind of following in the footsteps of Honey Dijon. This is one of the popular parties that even straight people will go to, and it's one of the only places that's more for club kids and has weird kids performing."

Batekoo:

"This party is based in São Paulo now, but it's originally from Salvador. To me, it's one of the most interesting things happening right now. It's very rare for a Black and Afro-Brazilian led movement to have such an impact in Brazil. Every color of the rainbow is represented here. People go to dance, and the kids who go have a very cool sense of fashion."

Europe

Athens, Greece

Most homos know Athens as nothing more than a stopover on the way to Mykonos, an island famous for its milky-white homes, marbled blue water, and fist-pumping muscle queens moshing to Loren Allred's "Never Enough" from 2017's box office hit *The Greatest Showman*. But before your next toga-themed circuit party in the Greek islands, consider extending your stay for a day or two in Athens. It turns out there's more to this city than just laying the foundations for all of Western civilization! According to locals, the city's LGBTQ scene is vibrant, weird, and growing—Sappho is probably composing a lyric poem in its honor as we speak.

Be Here, BEqueer in Athens

BEqueer is a collective that runs a popular LGBTQ bar in Athens. The space is home to some of the most famous drag queens in the country, who are known for performances that are equal parts weird and playful. They're also one of the reasons the collective behind the bar thinks the true heart of queer entertainment in Greece is on the mainland, and not the country's more famous island of sin, Mykonos.

Sassy Planet: Why did you found BEqueer?
BEqueer: We started BEqueer in November 2017 because we felt the need to create a venue in Athens where everyone could feel comfortable and safe, regardless of gender, sexuality, or identity. We were also fascinated by the emerging drag scene in Athens, so we really wanted to create a space for the performers we loved and to dedicate a night to them.

SP: What's the LGBTQ scene like in Athens, and how has it changed over the years?
BQ: We feel like we have some distance yet to cover before we'll have more inclusive spaces. Of course, it feels better than 20 years ago, for example, but we can still improve a lot. You must realize that Greece only recently legalized civil partnerships for same-sex couples, so there isn't full acceptance—especially for the less privileged, like trans people in our community (but

not just them). In Athens, you can never actually feel totally safe from verbal or physical abuse. Things seem to get a bit better over the decades, though. Young people today are less narrow-minded.

SP: Your most popular night is Friday, when you host a drag party—some of the lewks are amazing! Who are some of the queens that perform?
BQ: Thank you! Our resident drag queens are Chraja, Filothei, and Darla Qubit. Each one of them does something completely different, from campy, fun stuff to Broadway musicals. They also do a lot of experimental and underground material. They have complete freedom in how they express themselves onstage, so that's the most interesting part. They also regularly invite other performers or drag queens, so you never know what to expect. On Saturdays we invite local DJs, so for the most part each Saturday is also a bit different, but we're always focusing on a general pop-fun feeling.

SP: BEqueer has been described as friendly, open, and mixed (all genders, all sexualities, and so on). How have you created this kind of environment?
BQ: That was our goal from the beginning. We wanted the LGBTQI+ community to have a permanent home where they can feel safe and have fun. Of course, aside from our intentions,

the crowd really makes BEqueer what it is. It's very diverse and accepting, and the credit goes to them, but also the people we're collaborating with.

A partygoer at BEqueer.

SP: Most of the gays in New York are quick to go straight to Mykonos when visiting Greece. Should queer people be giving Athens more attention?
BQ: Of course queer people should be giving more attention to Athens—we feel that the scene is a lot more contemporary than in Mykonos. We understand that an island is the ideal place for a vacation, but the heart of queer entertainment beats in Athens. There's always stuff happening, but you usually find out about it through social media, so you just need to have your ears and eyes open. Often, parties aren't happening on a regular basis or at the same venue. For example, there's an emerging ballroom scene in Athens from the House of Kareola, which organizes vogue nights and galas from time to time.

Berlin, Germany

Whether it's stumbling upon real-life, just-sitting-there, like, *wow, actual* glory holes in the gay, nudist section of the Strandbad Wannsee swimming area, or wandering, also naked, through the subterranean labyrinth of Lab.Oratory (techno dream-club Berghain's underground gay sex mega-palace), Berlin has a well-earned reputation as an unabashedly—and sometimes clothing-optional—queer metropolis. But there's more to see here than just parties,

darkrooms, and sex dungeons. Berlin is a bastion of affordability and creativity in an otherwise affluent and sometimes overly polished Germany. And with a haunting past, and a present that not only attempts to deal with those mistakes but to keep their memory alive as long as possible, Berlin is a complex, ever-evolving jumble of history, horror, freedom, and livability—and an absolute must on any queer traveler's European itinerary.

Chat WITH A LOCAL

Sassy_Planet: From the Weimar-era Berlin immortalized in Christopher Isherwood's books, to the modern-day, sex-positive city and its seemingly infinite queer spaces, parties, and communities, Berlin has maintained its place as a gay mecca for nearly a hundred years. What is it about Berlin that attracts LGBTQ people from around the world?

Sammywammy: I think it's a combination of things. There's definitely that unique history, from the Isherwood time and before, when Berlin was a city with a large and relatively open gay scene—long before other major cities. And then that community was wiped out by the Nazis, but it came back during the period when West Berlin was like an island of lefty, freedom-loving people surrounded by East Germany.

Sammywammy: I think what really turned Berlin into a gay and LGBTQ mecca though happened in the 1990s, after the fall of the Berlin Wall and reunification, and the rise of techno culture, all-night clubs, and illegal parties in old factories and bunkers. The gay scene was incorporated into that, or was a big part of that, and that kind of mainstreamed gay culture into this scene, which became famous in the city and legendary across the world. I think part of that mixed underground culture also ushered in early forms of queer culture, since labels and identities were de-emphasized in a way, and people didn't have to be strictly gay or straight or gender normative. It was and is a scene that included everyone; the early Love Parades embodied this too. I think this image has been successfully promoted—and in many ways commodified—in present-day Berlin, in the club scene and nightlife world. I think you could say this is illustrated in the relationship between Berghain and Lab.Oratory.

Sassy_Planet: How so?

Sammywammy: Berghain isn't strictly gay, but there's a gay aesthetic there, for the image and for tourists to feel wild and alternative. And then right underneath is a large hardcore gay sex club that really *is* for gays.

Sammywammy: So I think this idea of Berlin being a gay mecca is really for the mainstream, mostly straight world, but LGBTQ people have benefited from this image in trickle-down ways, and perhaps have been harmed by it in other ways.

Sassy_Planet: There seem to be a handful of cities in the world, like Berlin and New Orleans, that gain a reputation for being cities of "lost boys." Do you have an opinion on what that means and why Berlin has this reputation?

Sammywammy: I don't know exactly why that happened with Berlin, but there are certainly examples of how that is part of the mythology and image of the city. The idea of (often gay) men leaving their countries to come to Berlin for a kind of secret, perhaps shameful, freedom, made famous by writers like Isherwood, as mentioned, is definitely part of it. But writings like his also seemed to describe a lot of the local Berlin boys as lost and alone, living in poverty in a city dealing with skyrocketing unemployment, and falling into male prostitution or other creative or desperate livelihoods. There was an idea that many Berlin boys—often portrayed as heterosexual but enthusiastically flexible for a price—were on their own in the world and trying to survive, while at the same time living in the moment and vainly entertaining fantasies about themselves and their futures. And then later, during the Cold War years, when young German men could avoid military service if they moved to West Berlin, there was literally an influx of romantic, lefty, lost German boys who came to the city in search of alternative lives, separated from their families and old lives by the Wall and their political ideas.

Sammywammy: I think these images and themes continued to inspire people to come to Berlin. And I think it's one of the reasons Berlin has exploded with lost boys—and girls—from other places over the last 15 years, to the extent that it has now very much become a city of people who are *not* lost, but rather who have flocked to a famous city known as the world center of alternative culture, and who know exactly what they're doing. In that way, I think Berlin has outgrown that reputation.

Sassy_Planet: What are Berlin's different queer neighborhoods like?

Sammywammy: There are a lot of differences [between them], but I guess the main neighborhood is Schöneberg, which is the classic gay district. It's older, more insulated, more focused on sex and cruising and drugs, and fetish and sex tourism. It's the area you can walk around holding hands with your boyfriend and never worry about getting negative looks or comments. If you want to have that feeling of, like, "this is our area," then that's the place for you. Whenever the big Pride or fetish festivals come to town, this is where they're centered.

Sassy_Planet: How about Kreuzberg and Neukölln?

Sammywammy: Kreuzberg and Neukölln, and by extension Friedrichshain and Mitte, and in the past Prenzlauer Berg, all offer the alternative: an LGBTQ presence and integration within the larger scene. And even more appealing for many people is the fact that, in these areas, the clubs, cafés, and bars that are officially or mainly LGBTQ are respected, and also frequented, by straight people. These areas show what I think Berlin is really known for: the normalization of queer culture in many central parts of the city, as well as a real respect for queer culture. This scene also represents more current styles and music. A lot of queer people in Berlin prefer to be in spaces like that, most often gay men, and they like the option to be able to run back to Schöneberg and Nollendorfplatz for all the comforts and guilty pleasures.

Queer History: INSTITUT FÜR SEXUALWISSENSCHAFT

The Institut für Sexualwissenschaft, or Institute for Sexology, was founded by Magnus Hirschfeld in Berlin in 1919. The groundbreaking sexology clinic pioneered gender affirmation treatments and procedures for transgender people, as well as the study of human sexuality outside heterosexual practice. The clinic ran for roughly 14 years, serving thousands of patients of all gender identities and sexual orientations. It was sadly shuttered permanently by the Nazis in 1933, and its publications, library and archives were publicly burned.

Juan Ramos is Living the Berlin Life You Wish You Had

Connecticut-born Juan Ramos has lived in Berlin since he was 22 (he is now 31). Since moving there, he's worked in the city spinning and producing various forms of electronic music. He's a resident DJ at Cocktail d'Amore, one of Berlin's most infamous queer and sex-positive dance parties, and in 2019 released his debut album, *Changing Hands*, which he describes as a mixture of "jarring textures, incomplete phrases, and circus-like abstractions of pop culture."

Sassy Planet: Tell us about you, Juan.
Juan Ramos: I was born and grew up in Connecticut. While I would have liked to have stayed in the US, I knew that the fight to even get a foot in the door as a DJ would be more than just an uphill battle. I ended up finding myself in a relationship with someone in Berlin, and it opened the opportunity for me to come here and dive headfirst into what was, and in many respects still is, the most active scene in the world for club culture. Over the years since, I've primarily lived in Kreuzberg, working as a DJ and producer.

SP: Describe the LGBTQ DJ scene in Berlin and how it's unique.
JR: What sets the scene apart here is its size. There really is a space for everyone, so there's not much feeling of competition or animosity like there tends to be in cities with smaller scenes. A lot of DJs from different parties are all friends and get on very well with one another and are supportive of each other's endeavors. This also lends itself to many of us being able to take a lot of creative risks—because we know there's a support network behind us, and the cost of living is still relatively reasonable. I would be remiss if I didn't mention that the city does do its fair share to cater both financially and politically to its culture sector, which has helped create this vibrant diversity for artists to live in.

SP: What's your favorite party in Berlin?
JR: This is of course a biased answer—though if I had to think about it objectively I think I would still come to the same conclusion. For me the best queer event is still Cocktail d'Amore. Outside of my being intimately part of the event, I've always held an appreciation for what it has added to the culture here in Berlin. There's a whole other, and dare I say more interesting, part of Berlin that slightly fewer people get to appreciate, and that's the part of the culture that Cocktail really caters to. The drag queens, baby dykes, leather daddies, and nonbinary people can intermingle and, in essence, appreciate what one another have to bring to what are fundamentally social experiments being soundtracked by club music. It then becomes much less about dressing the right way and more about letting your freak flag fly and being honest with the world around you about who and what you are, without fear of judgment.

And while I say that Cocktail is my favorite, I'd also like to point out the incredible contribution that our brothers [who run the party] Buttons have done in being true community leaders. They've put their hearts into providing a space for queer people not just to party and exist freely, but also for them to thrive and have resources to help address the issues that we face as a community here in Berlin.

Top 10 Thangs to Do in Berlin

1.  EiNS

Swim in one of the city's many lakes during the summer. Schlachtensee, Wannsee, and Teufelsee are some that draw queer crowds. Berlin comes alive in the warmer months, and everyone ends up at the lakes.

2. ZWEi

Berghain. Duh. The most overstimulating and spiritual dance club experience you'll ever have, with a legendarily exclusive door policy. Tips for getting in: Wear black, don't speak English, don't arrive in a huge group, and look as gay as possible. Some think having a stamp from last night's fun at Lab.Oratory helps you get in. Also, research the DJ lineup in advance, and if the bouncers give you trouble, tell them you're here to see so-and-so spin and they just might give you mercy. If you don't get in, don't sulk—you're in Berlin!

(1)

(2)

3. DREi

Lab.Oratory. Not for the faint of heart. Prepare to watch 900 naked gay men fuck, fist-fuck, suck, and piss on one another to the tunes of amazing DJs in a spooky, impressively constructed space meant to evoke an early to mid-twentieth-century laboratory, with plumbing designed specifically for piss play. It's located in the basement beneath Berghain but is much easier to get into. Generally allows gay men only.

4.  ViER

Berlin is a city of monthly and seasonal queer parties. In summer especially, check with a local to find out what's going on while you're in town. In recent years, parties like Buttons and Cocktail d'Amore have delivered incredible outdoor experiences.

5.  FÜNF

Check out the iconic gayborhood of Schöneberg (think bears, gay elders, tourists, twinks, and window shopping for XL butt plugs). Even the neighborhood's Nollendorfplatz U-Bahn station is rainbow-themed. Enjoy a beer at Prinzknecht or Tom's.

6. SECHS

Have a drink at one of Kreuzberg and Neukölln's mainstay LGBTQ bars: Rose's for kitschy and cozy; Möbel-Olfe for hip, intellectual and smoky; and Silver Future for young, queer, and lively.

7. SIEBEN

Head to the Landwehr Canal in Kreuzberg or Neukölln. Spot a bevy of swans in its waters, check out its grassy banks populated by groups of friends drinking beer in warm weather, and wander its bordering streets, host to Turkish and eclectic food markets.

(3)

8. ACHT

Take a jog, fly a kite, or just hang out at Tempelhofer Feld, a functioning airport up until 2008 and now a gigantic public park with a big open sky above it. Stand in the middle of the runway and take a sunset selfie.

9. NEUN

Enjoy an amazing meal at Max und Moritz, a traditional German restaurant opened in 1902 on Oranienstrasse in Kreuzberg. Think spätzle, sausages, and beer from heaven. Prepare to like German food after this.

(4)

10. ZEHN

Take in the history. Berlin is a vibrant city with a dark past. Pause to read an inscription on one of the thousands of bronze *Stolpersteine* ("stumbling stones") that dot the sidewalks, which mark the residences of individuals—largely Jewish, but also many homosexual, Black, or disabled—who were persecuted or exterminated by the Nazi regime. Explore the undulating columns and alleyways of the Memorial to the Murdered Jews of Europe (and maybe don't take an insensitive selfie). Or take a day trip to Sachsenhausen, the former concentration camp outside the city. Prepare to be moved by images of the Jews, gays, lesbians, and others who were imprisoned and killed there.

1: Berghain, with Lab.Oratory lurking underneath.
2: The Nollendorfplatz U-Bahn station with its rainbow hues. 3: Crowds hanging out by the Landwehr Canal. 4: Tempelhofer Feld.

Bologna, Italy

Italy can be a confusing one for queer tourists: a central European country with incredible history and food culture, filled with passionate pasta-eating, cigarette-smoking, Vespa-riding heartthrobs, and yet it has one of the lowest LGBTQ rights quotients of any country in the region. Even Rome, Italy's largest city, is surprisingly not its gayest metropolis. Why is this? Well, in short, Catholicism. Compared to the rest of Italy's cities, though, Milan and Bologna are its shining queer stars. This is where it gets surprising—yes, Bologna, only the seventh most populous city in Italy, is considered by many to be its gayest. A medieval university town whose streets are flanked by an incredible network of porticoes (covered sidewalks), Bologna boasts an incredibly rich LGBTQ community within the context of a mid-sized historic city. Hint: it's kind of like Florence, but with gays instead of tourists.

RED to Filth by Matteo Giorgi

Matteo Giorgi, who was born and raised in Bologna, is the art director of RED, an LGBTQ organization focused on improving gay and trans life in Italy. RED is also charged with co-producing the annual Bologna Pride party and parade. The group additionally organizes events that draw people from across Europe, thanks to performances from world-renowned DJs and drag acts.

Sassy Planet: What's your queer contribution to Bologna, Matteo?
Matteo Giorgi: I started working at Cassero, the oldest Italian LGBT association, in 2003. In the 11 years I worked there I did a lot of fantastic things: I was an organizer of some special parties, an art director, and a host of national Pride in 2008 and 2012. I was also director of *Cassero* magazine and the head of communications for the [Cassero queer arts] association. Since 2014 I've been the art director of RED, the other big gay association in Bologna.

SP: What's RED all about?
MG: RED has become one of the most important faces of Italian gay culture. We work in two different ways: politically, preparing campaigns online and around the city, and organizing the Bologna Pride party and parade every year; and then we have the "disco" side of our operation. Every Saturday we have big, more commercial parties where people come from all over the country. We were the first to bring drag stars from *RuPaul's Drag Race* to Italy. Then there's the more hardcore nightlife side of what we do, with dancers and DJs from all over the world and from big parties like Circuit Festival [in Barcelona] and La Demence [in Brussels]. We were also the first to bring Eliad Cohen and the PAPA PARTY to Italy.

SP: Bologna isn't on most queer travelers' Italian itineraries—why is it worth a visit?
MG: Because Bologna is the city of culture and freedom. It's a small city, so if you stay for two days you can see everything. You can breathe in Italian gay culture on every street, everywhere. You really can be whoever you want. And the food! Bologna recently won a prize as the city with the best food in the world. A lot of carbs are waiting for you! Cassero and Arcigay, two of the largest gay organizations in Italy, both have headquarters in Bologna. We're a city of culture—we have what's considered the oldest university in the world (and it's still one of the most important in Europe), and we also have one of the world's most important film archives, the Cineteca di Bologna. So if you love cinema, culture, and freedom, you're an ideal visitor to our city.

SP: What are your favorite queer spots in Bologna?
MG: Bologna is very strange, because you don't find gay bars here: you find gays in every bar, in every place. You can get a beer in a small bar and

(1)

then hang out on the rocks in Piazza San Francesco or Piazza Verdi, or take a walk to all the bars along Via del Pratello. Every bar, party, and place can become the perfect LGBT situation. Some special mentions: Bart Club has been Bologna's cruising spot for 30 years. You can't stay in Bologna without meeting Flavio, the bearded owner of the club. And then PLUS is the one and only Italian organization for HIV-positive people, headquartered here in Bologna. It's an organization that helps people with HIV testing, counseling, hotlines, seminars, and workshops.

SP: What about the Bologna of the past? There seem to be some myths and legends.
MG: I have to tell you about two in particular. Michelino is the first. It was a big parking lot that was very famous in the 1980s and '90s, where everyone in the city met when there wasn't Grindr or smartphones. It was the biggest cruising area of the city, and during summer you could find all

the gay guys hanging out there, chatting and laughing, and not just looking for a fuck.

The second is Vipera. It was a gay club in Bologna that was very famous in the 1990s for about five years. At the entrance was the iconic Marcella di Folco, one of the first prominent trans public figures in Italy, who had also acted in some Federico Fellini movies. She was really crazy,

(2)

and if she liked you you could come in; otherwise you had to stay outside. So after a few weeks of her working the door, people started bringing sofas right up to the door of the club, and they hung out just to see what Marcella would be doing that night at the door, and of course

laughing at what she'd say to those she didn't let in. She was one of the most important people for Bologna and she represented who we are. Unfortunately, we lost her almost 10 years ago.

SP: What does it mean to be an LGBTQ person in Italy?
MG: It's not possible to give a simple answer about what it is to be gay in Italy as a whole. You can see it by traveling around with Grindr: when you're in the big cities of the north, you'll see

(3)

a Grindr full of smiling faces; if you go to the south or to smaller cities, it's only blank profiles. Politics is not helping us. We've only had civil unions for four years—I got married in New York because I can't in Italy— and we don't have laws against homophobia. But maybe some things are changing. The last Bologna Pride was full of young people that see the truth. They are the future. And this is the only future that is possible.

1: XXL Night at RED. 2: Marcella Di Folco at Bologna Pride in 2008. 3: The RED crew, including Matteo Giorgi in the front row with black jacket.

Matteo Giorgi's
Top Bologna To-Dos for Ho-Mos

Le Due Torri

"Visit the famous Due Torri, the two medieval leaning towers."

Splendido

"Go to this party, which takes place at Comodo."

Walk the Portico di San Luca

"It's a path of 666 arches leading to a hilltop church, making it the longest covered walkway on earth."

Visit MAMbo

"The city's modern art museum."

Al Cambio

"Eat here for the best tagliatelle, lasagne, and tortellini in the city."

Lisbon, Portugal

It feels like, only a few years ago, Lisbon was not a city that featured on many international travelers' lists. Now, suddenly everyone's eating *pastéis de nata* and planning their early retirement in Portugal. Lisbon has recently opened up to tourists in a totally new way, all the while still somehow holding on to its charm and authenticity. Whether you're wandering the winding, narrow streets of the historic Alfama neighborhood or partying all night at LuxFrágil, one of the most incredible nightclubs in all of Europe, Lisbon will hit you hard. But as a queer traveler, you might need to dig a bit deeper than in other Iberian cities like Madrid or Barcelona to find your LGBTQ sistren.

Príncipe Real is known as the city's gay neighborhood, but its streets are mostly residential, romantic, and quiet—a far cry from anything like a Chueca in Madrid or a Soho in London. But queer history runs deep in Lisbon. One of the country's foremost pop heroes was none other than António Variações, an openly gay musical genius of the 1980s, complete with bleached-blond mustache and experimental future-hipster fashion sense. He's so popular that his biopic, *Variações*, was the highest-grossing film in Portugal when it was released in 2019. Sadly, like so many others, Variações died of AIDS-related complications in 1984, at the age of 39.

Alex d'Alva Teixeira on Lisbon's Alt-Pop Music Scene

Alex d'Alva Teixeira was born in Angola but has lived in Lisbon since he was just a year old. He is a member of the indie pop band D'ALVA, which is on a mission to promote diversity and inclusion in Portugal's local music scene.

Sassy Planet: Hi, Alex! Describe Lisbon for us, and tell us a bit about your background.
Alex d'Alva Teixeira: I'd say that most areas of this city are pretty progressive and liberal. Lots of queer people move here so they can live among other like-minded individuals. In other areas that aren't as cosmopolitan, Portugal tends to be more conservative, but there are exceptions, like Porto, for example.

I can only speak about my personal experience. My parents are immigrants from São Tomé and Brazil. When I was younger, Lisbon seemed a bit distant due to my parents' overprotective nature and the conservative education they gave me. When I became an adult, I was able to spend more time in the city and meet more people like myself. I grew up in a small town that's only 18 miles from Lisbon. I always saw the capital as a place filled with hope and promise, where I was sure I'd be able to live freely and be myself, not only because I'd meet other queer people in LGBTQ+-friendly spaces, but also because I'd be able to find more work opportunities as an artist. Nowadays, I feel like people tend to be more respectful of non-heteronormative ways of living. Even if they don't agree with or support it, they probably won't be rude or violent toward you.

I'm part of a pop band called D'ALVA. Since the very beginning, people could tell that inclusion and diversity were among our core values and beliefs. We like to think of our music as something that anyone can listen to, as opposed to being elitist about it. We've had the chance to play at events promoted by the government and the city mayor, because they try their best to portray Lisbon as a diverse city where everyone is welcome—and that's actually true.

SP: Do a lot of LGBTQ people leave Lisbon to move to bigger cities?
AT: Lisbon is obviously very small compared to other European cities. Bigger cities with a larger population tend to have more like-minded people, more opportunities, and also more LGBTQ+-friendly spaces. I have friends who moved out of the country looking for better work opportunities, but also looking for an alternative way to live their sexuality. Some of them also feel some degree of shame in living their sexuality among their peers and families, so they move to a bigger city to get a fresh start with new people. Some just go after a broader experience in a bigger place with more to offer. But I feel that if you're in Lisbon you don't need to "run away" to live freely, and at the same time you know that you're having a small-scale experience. Still, if you're a gay, white, cis male, you'll be fine, because the vast majority of

queer spaces here cater to people like you.

SP: What makes queer life in Lisbon unique compared to other cities?
AT: I feel like other cities might have bigger venues, and also a lot more diversity: even if you're looking for small, niche stuff, any niche will be bigger in a larger city, so you'll have more options. Still, you can manage to have tons of fun here in Lisbon. We have at least one or two gay hotels and resorts, a few gay bars and nightclubs, a few saunas, steam rooms, and sex clubs; we even have a gay beach. Also, due to the fact that the country has a very conservative past, you have several cruising spots where men meet secretly if they don't want to do it out in the open. I'm glad I live in a country where I can live my sexuality freely, and in that regard Portugal isn't as dangerous as other countries. And some

tourists even say that Lisbon in general can be more liberal than certain areas of London.

SP: What are your favorite LGBTQ parties, events, or spaces in Lisbon?
AT: [Since I only came out publicly last year] I've only attended some parties and clubs that are LGBTQ+-friendly, rather than necessarily focused on the LGBTQ+ community. I haven't yet had the chance to go to Trumps, the most popular (and official) gay nightclub in Lisbon. Luckily, nightclubs like LuxFrágil or even Musicbox are very friendly and welcoming, and that's sort of how I managed to go out in Lisbon for almost 10 years without feeling the need to go to exclusively LGBTQ+ venues—because there are other places where you're not only welcome but also encouraged to be yourself, without fear or reservation. I'll definitely be

(1)

(2)

going to nightclubs like Trumps or Construction [soon], mostly because I've never been to a gay nightclub before. I also need to go to Finalmente, which is the oldest venue in town and has drag shows. It's a local classic and kind of a mandatory place to visit at least once.

SP: Portugal was under an authoritarian dictatorship for more than 40 years, until the mid-1970s—a time when gay pride started gaining popularity elsewhere around the Western world. That must have had an impact on things. Do you know of any stories about how gay life used to be in Lisbon?

AT: I was born in the 1990s, so most of the stories I've heard relate to small bars that you'd get into by saying a password, or which were very discreet and secretive; but those don't seem to exist that much anymore. But if you learn about the most iconic gay venues like Trumps or Finalmente, you'll realize that these spaces are intimately connected to stories of resistance, and also had an important impact on our national pop culture.

Apart from the gay beach, there's also Parque Eduardo VII, which used to be, and still kind of is, a well-known cruising spot. And outside Lisbon, for example, there's a small wooded area in Queluz that used to be a hunting ground (as far as I know) where people can go for walks, and where gay men hook up and do their thing in the bushes.

1 & 2: Alex d'Alva Teixeira's band D'ALVA.

London, UK

London boasts the sort of diverse, sprawling, multifaceted, and hyper-specific queer scene that only exists in a handful of places worldwide. Beyond Soho's campy queens and Vauxhall's beefy bears are East London's queer artists and weirdos. And while the city's powerful real estate industry relentlessly attempts to turn East London into one gigantic glass-box luxury condo, a vibrant and creative culture persists here—in spite of the tragic closure of several beloved LGBTQ spaces in the area in recent years.

Stephen Isaac-Wilson Says Go East, Young Queer

Stephen Isaac-Wilson is a London-based filmmaker and artist. His work has been exhibited at museums and galleries including Tate Britain, Barbican Art Gallery, the Serpentine Gallery, and Victoria Miro. He also creates documentaries, music videos, and commercials. Most recently, Stephen collaborated on a project celebrating the influence of queer artist Ajamu X and examining the Black Pervert's Network sex parties he ran in the 1990s.

Sassy Planet: Give us the mini Stephen bio.
Stephen Isaac-Wilson: I'm from South London but have lived all around the capital, and now live in the east. I'm lucky enough to be a full-time filmmaker.

SP: London is huge, with so many queer areas and things to do. Where do you hang out the most?
SIW: I find myself mostly in the east, where I live: Hackney, Dalston, Stoke Newington. I like green spaces, so I make the most of the outdoors around me. The queer scene in these areas is good too, and probably the strongest in the capital. The majority of the area is gay-friendly, but there are also explicitly queer spaces such as The Queen Adelaide pub and Dalston Superstore.

SP: What are your fave gay spaces and things in London?
SIW: It's mostly just where my friends are: cute [queer club] nights like PDA, or warehouse parties in South London or Tottenham. I also love outdoor drinking spaces in Soho, swimming in [the outdoor ponds in] Hampstead Heath, and hanging out in Hackney Marshes.

Hampstead Heath.

Stephen Isaac-Wilson's
Top London To-Dos for Ho-Mos

Try different cuisines

"In East London I'd recommend Peppers & Spice, Troy Bar, and All Nations for Caribbean food; Mangal 1 for Turkish; and Sông Quê for Vietnamese."

Make Hackney your base

"Then rent or borrow a bike to ride into Central London."

Check out some art

"Go to the Tate Modern, the ICA, and the Barbican Centre (which has an amazing conservatory)."

Wander the city

"Walk down Brick Lane during the day and along the South Bank at night."

Enjoy the green spaces

"Go to Regent's Park, London Fields, Victoria Park, and Clissold Park."

The Closure of East London's Gay Pubs

There was a time, not long ago, when East London was home to three of the best queer pubs in all of the UK, each located within a five-minute walk of one another. And then, within the course of a few months, they all closed amidst a tidal wave of neighborhood gentrification. These pubs were The Joiners Arms (1997–2015), the Nelson's Head (2007–14), and The George & Dragon (2002–15). The Joiners Arms, smack in the middle of a residential strip of Hackney Road, had a dancefloor that lit up on weekends, an incredibly mixed queer clientele, a tiny smoke-filled patio, and dependably good DJs. The Nelson's Head was a proper English pub with a tastefully queer aesthetic, where everyone inside wore plaid, had a beard, and looked like fantasy English boyfriend material. The George & Dragon, a charmingly cluttered neighborhood gem, was nestled on a V-shaped plot of land and looked as if it had remained unchanged, inside and out, for the past hundred years (even if it had only been a gay pub for a little more than a decade). However, one of these venues, The Joiners Arms, became an international example of how to protect our vulnerable queer spaces, even if they've already been shuttered.

Immediately following the Joiners' closure due to property development, a group of East London queers quickly banded together, calling themselves Friends of the Joiners Arms. They successfully petitioned local government to deem the closed space an "asset of community value." According to the organization's website, "After a long hard battle, in late 2017, the Tower Hamlets council granted permission to develop the site as long as the following conditions were met: a pub must be included in the new development, which should be run as an LGBTQI+ venue with a lease of 25 years, and with opening hours mirroring those of the original pub. Further, the developers

The Joiners Arms, circa 2012.

should pay for the first year's rent and contribute to the fit-out costs of the new venue."

Quite a turnaround—and all due to queers self-organizing and recognizing their right to spaces of their own. At the time of writing this book, no such LGBTQI+ venue has yet opened on the site of the Joiners. But the ability of East London queers to stop a corporate developer serves as an example that these spaces are protectable, important, and worth fighting for.

Dalston Superstore:
Known as a beacon of all things queer in East
London, Dalston Superstore regularly hosts
club nights, drag brunches, and art exhibtions.
Pictured here are performers and revelers at the
venue's Club Tantrum and Mints parties.

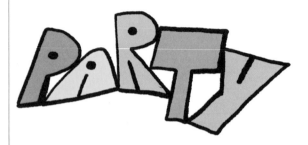

(2)

(1)

(3)

(4)

(6)

(5)

(7)

1: Lexy. 2: Pinky Bitz. 3: Josephine Jones.
4: Milk Shandy. 5: Sophie Brain. 6: Nadia B. Juma.
7: Kuntessa and The People's Pwincess.

Madrid, Spain

Madrid is one of those cities that doesn't necessarily bring an easily identifiable landmark to mind, unlike Barcelona's Sagrada Familia or Rome's Colosseum. And while the city's Prado Museum is one of the most highly regarded art spaces in the world, Madrid sometimes feels like an adorable throwback town, with old-man tailor shops and siesta culture often in full view. The city, technically one of the largest in Europe, feels truly local and effortlessly authentic in contrast with its rival Barcelona, which is often criticized for pandering too much to international tourism. Oh, and Madrid is really, really gay. Like, surprisingly gay. Like, everyone is gay. Everywhere. Especially in Chueca.

Chat WITH A LOCAL

Sassy_Planet: People see Chueca as the quintessential European gayborhood. Is there more to Madrid's gay scene, though?

Samantha_Hudson: I think nowadays the whole city is gay. You see queer people everywhere. But personally, [I feel] the scene can be a bit heteronormative sometimes. Madrid needs more club kids. More monsters. More freaks. A lot of the club owners are trapped in the 2000s, with a very concrete stereotype of what a drag performer is. But, step by step, a new scene is emerging, and it feels more diverse. It's organized by young queer people.

Samantha_Hudson: But yes, in Chueca there are these pubs that have been there forever, with these old-lady drag queens who perform every night, impersonating the greatest divas of Spanish music like Lola Flores and Isabel Pantoja. But I think that's the charm of the area. Chueca still has the most iconic clubs, and if you want to go do something gay on a weeknight, places in Chueca are always open.

An El Puñal Dorao party.

Sassy_Planet: What's your favorite party in Madrid?

Samantha_Hudson: El Puñal Dorao. The party has kind of a ballroom scene and it happens every few months, each time with a different theme. There's a runway show where a winner is crowned, and the vibe is very inclusive. The DJs and the music are mostly techno and electronic.

Sassy_Planet: A lot of people's first exposure to queer Spain is via Pedro Almodóvar films. Is his influence still very strong in LGBTQ Madrid?

Samantha_Hudson: Yes, he's one of our more precious treasures. During the 1980s, Spain went through a very rich artistic and cultural moment. A lot of good musicians and performers, and tons of mesmerizing looks and outfits—people like Fabio McNamara, Alaska y Dinarama, and Ana Curra, for example. For me at least, that era is still influencing us.

A dancer at El Puñal Dorao.

Paris, France

Berets are widely recognized as the gayest form of hat (or *chapeau*, if you're nasty), so it should come as no surprise that Paris is among the biggest *centres de la vie homosexuelle* in Europe. Le Marais, stretched through the 3rd and 4th arrondissements, has historically been the heart of queer Paris. But the entire French capital—from Oscar Wilde's tomb in Père Lachaise Cemetery to those adorable little fruitcakes sold in all the patisseries—is pretty gaiiii.

Chat WITH A LOCAL

Sassy_Planet: What's something super gay about Paris that you wouldn't find just by Googling?

MecParis: Paris is so gay! There are lots of little hidden things. There's a plaque on rue Montorgueil that hardly anyone knows about that commemorates a young couple who were executed there in the eighteenth century for being gay. And there's Legay Choc, a boulangerie that makes baguettes shaped like dicks.

Sassy_Planet: *Délicieuse!* What about nightlife?

MecParis: Le Marais is still the main gay area, but it's changing. There are still lots of gay bars there; some have been there for a long time now, like the Duplex, Cox, and Open Café. But now the gay bars are competing with all the little fancy boutiques and shops. It's kind of like SoHo in New York. The queers made it cool, and now they're being pushed out.

Sassy_Planet: So does the city feel less gay than it used to?

Legay Choc boulangerie.

MecParis: In some ways, yes. There may be fewer bars than there once were, but there's also more activism and awareness. In June 2019, to mark the 50th anniversary of the Stonewall riots, the city renamed four blocks after different famous queer events or advocates. We also have far more lesbian bars than lots of other European cities, which I think is cool.

Paris' Gay Marais

In June 2019, the city of Paris renamed three squares and one street in the 4th arrondissement—which encompasses Le Marais, the center of gay life there—after queer events and advocates:

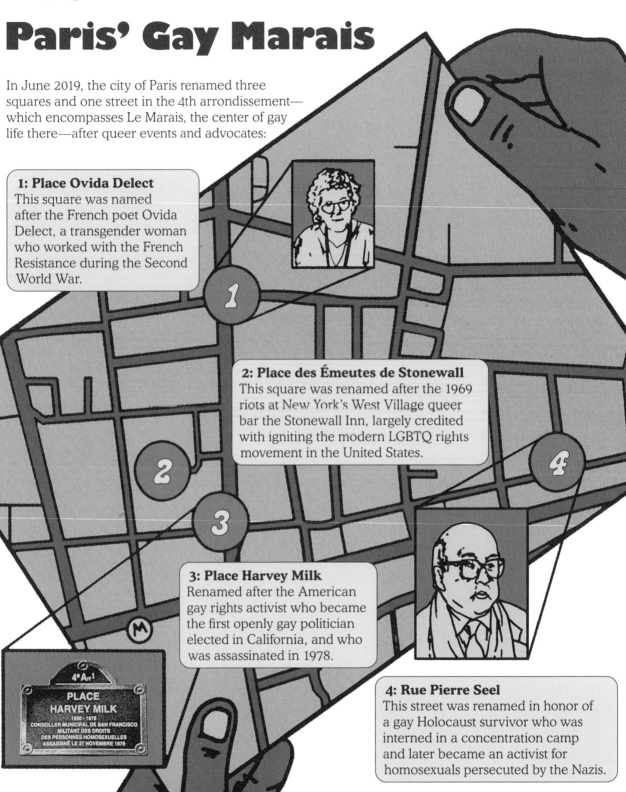

1: Place Ovida Delect
This square was named after the French poet Ovida Delect, a transgender woman who worked with the French Resistance during the Second World War.

2: Place des Émeutes de Stonewall
This square was renamed after the 1969 riots at New York's West Village queer bar the Stonewall Inn, largely credited with igniting the modern LGBTQ rights movement in the United States.

3: Place Harvey Milk
Renamed after the American gay rights activist who became the first openly gay politician elected in California, and who was assassinated in 1978.

4: Rue Pierre Seel
This street was renamed in honor of a gay Holocaust survivor who was interned in a concentration camp and later became an activist for homosexuals persecuted by the Nazis.

The Lesbian Bars
of Gai Paris

La Mutinerie

Good for: Drinks and fun, inclusive vibes.
With a feminist library, the bar (whose name
means "the mutiny") is like a community
center where you can get drunk.

Le Bar'Ouf

Good for: Day drinking, board games,
and pool. A bit stricter about catering
to female-identifying patrons only.

3W Kafé

Good for: Theme nights and karaoke.

La Champmeslé

Good for: Experiencing the oldest lesbian bar still
operating in Paris (it opened in the 1970s).

Le So What

Good for: Experiencing a lesbian bar
that doesn't even open until 11pm.

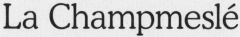

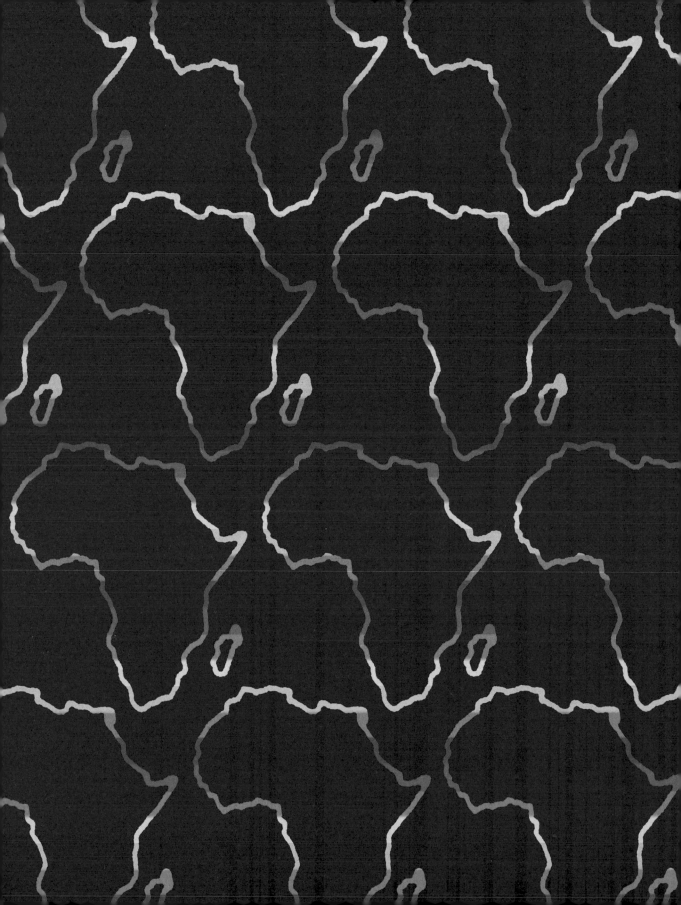

Accra, Ghana

Homosexuality has been criminalized in Ghana since the 1860s. And although the government hasn't actively prosecuted anyone for engaging in same-sex relations here in recent years, the queer community still faces discrimination and violence. Despite the fact that local LGBTQ advocates continue to press for rights and recognition, any semblance of an active scene remains very much underground. However, while chatting with locals in Accra—the country's capital and largest city—we found one exception to this rule. During the weeklong Chale Wote Street Art Festival, the LGBTQ community becomes slightly more visible.

 **WITH A LOCAL**

Sassy_Planet: What's the LGBTQ scene like in Ghana?

AccraDILF7000: The scene is fairly diverse, but not heavily organized in any particular way. Most people have their personal queer circles or private parties. General attitudes are not supportive, but queer life seems to be more visible now. I don't feel unsafe most of the time, although I also pass as straight a lot. Police will generally not use homosexuality as a pretext to impede your rights.

Sassy_Planet: Are you out?

AccraDILF7000: I'm pretty out personally, but not really at work. Homosexuality is still heavily frowned upon culturally because of colonial values. There are some intense anti-gay sentiments and misplaced religious zealots. In general, privilege provides a lot of insulation and peace of mind.

Sassy_Planet: When's the best time for a visit to Accra?

AccraDILF7000: I would say August, for Chale Wote. It's a full week of festivities.

Chale Wote Street Art Festival

Every year, Chale Wote Street Art Festival explodes onto the streets of Jamestown, an old colonial part of Accra, during the last week of August. The event brings together a dizzying array of local artists, dancers, fashion designers, musicians, actors, and more, who gather to participate in what the organizers, an art collective known as ACCRA [dot] ALT, call an "experimental platform." As the group explains on its website: "The artists use the festival to provoke. To soften old, conservative, crusted patterns of thought and to direct them into new paths. The art should encourage [people] to reflect. It should create inspiration. In addition to the artistic aspect the event also serves as a breeding ground for new political approaches."

Queers love any opportunity to soften crusted patterns, and Chale Wote is no different. While not by any means a "gay" festival, the local LGBTQ community is, comparatively speaking, out and open during the week of Chale Wote. Local journalist Kwasi Gyamfi Asiedu, writing in an article for *Quartz Africa* after 2019's festival, said that despite Ghana's anti-LGBTQ laws, and homosexuality generally being frowned upon both in the country and the city of Accra, he saw "women dance suggestively with each other" and described a scene where "a man wearing a rainbow train and a vertical ponytail trie[d] to weave through the crowd, [and was] abruptly stopped by festival revelers for photographs."

Despite this week of relatively open LGBTQ revelry, the local gay scene remains very much underground the rest of the year. "Outside the confines of this festival," Kwasi wrote, "the mob stopping to pose with rainbow-vertical-ponytail-man could be the same ones turning on him the next Monday if he walked on the streets dressed like that."

Acts of "unnatural carnal knowledge"—basically anything involving penetrative sex that's not with a vagina—are illegal in Ghana and punishable by up to three years in prison. According to a 2018 report by Human Rights Watch, this law is rarely if ever enforced, but LGBTQ people are still often the victims of violence and discrimination. However, for at least one week every year, Accra is out and proud.

Cairo, Egypt

LGBTQ culture in Cairo has experienced many starts and stops over the past few decades. While the community here has always largely existed in the shadows, gathering spaces were once more visible than they are today. The infamous Cairo 52 incident in 2001, during which 52 men were arrested onboard the floating gay nightclub Queen Boat on the Nile river for "obscene behavior," helped force the scene underground.

Egypt's revolution in 2011, which resulted in the overthrow of Hosni Mubarak's presidency, helped usher in a new generation of LGBTQ activists and visibility in Cairo. This, in turn, has sparked a backlash by the government of Abdel Fattah el-Sisi, most notably in 2017, when seven Egyptians were arrested at a Mashrou' Leila concert for "promoting homosexuality" by waving a rainbow flag.

Chat WITH A LOCAL

Sassy_Planet: What was it like growing up gay in Cairo?

CairoGuy: Egypt isn't what it was in previous years. When I was growing up, there was a semblance of queer space—clubs, bars, and other friendly spaces that weren't exactly "gay," but which were gay-friendly. This has changed a lot in the last 15 years or so, first after the notable Queen Boat incident, and then following the Arab Spring, which was followed by a massive crackdown. Homosexuality isn't criminalized in Egypt, but it falls under a public indecency law that can result in long prison sentences. Even the online scene has been impossible because cops are constantly catfishing in order to arrest people. So, Grindr no longer provides the opportunities it once yielded. Even worse, there's now a culture of informants, so fake profiles are hard to recognize as potential traps. It's truly depressing.

Sassy_Planet: How have things been in recent years for the LGBTQ community?

CairoGuy: The most important moment that really made things hit rock bottom was the Mashrou' Leila concert that took place in Cairo a few years ago. It's a Lebanese band with two openly gay members. A rainbow flag was raised mid-concert and that resulted in the band being barred [from playing in Egypt] for life, and the arrest of more than 50 concertgoers. Sarah Hegazi, the young woman who raised the flag, was later arrested and tortured in Cairo. She finally got asylum in Canada in 2019 but later sadly committed suicide. Her death didn't have much of an effect in Egypt [but] it generated some debate abroad. All this is to say that the situation is a bit tense, and no one would really have much of a positive spin on gay life in Egypt right now.

Sassy_Planet: Does any semblance of gay culture persist, then?

CairoGuy: Gay culture has always existed and will always exist in Egypt! You can simply look at the homoerotic dynamics that continue to dominate the streets of Cairo. Or the fact that gay weddings between men occurred in Siwa until the mid-twentieth century, until they were, ironically, banned by the British! From what I personally know, the gay scene today has shifted very underground, mostly into people's homes. But that doesn't prevent the possibility of encounters anywhere in the city. Some of the city's hotels are still famous cruising grounds, for example.

Queer History:
MASHROU' LEILA CONCERT

In 2017, the popular Lebanese band Mashrou' Leila—whose lead singer, Hamed Sinno, is openly gay—traveled to Cairo to perform in what would become their largest concert ever, with 35,000 people in attendance. In an act of defiance against the Egyptian government's aggressive stance on LGBTQ rights in recent years, several concertgoers were photographed waving rainbow pride flags while the group performed. Images went viral online, with many applauding the show's attendees for their pro-LGBTQ stance. However, the act landed seven Egyptians in prison for openly "promoting sexual deviancy."

One of those arrested was Sarah Hegazi, a 30-year-old Egyptian LGBTQ rights activist. She was later granted asylum in Canada after being jailed and tortured in her home country. In June 2020, she tragically took her own life. Following her death, one of the band's members, Haig Papazian, wrote an opinion article for the *New York Times* honoring her act of bravery. "That Ms. Hegazi felt safe enough to honor our music with her bravery is thrilling," he wrote. "That such a simple act forever altered and then ended her life brings me great sorrow. That plummet— from hope to despair— is familiar to anyone who dared to believe in the Arab Spring."

Hamed Sinno.

Cape Town, South Africa

Situated at the bottom tip of a vast continent that is definitely not renowned for its pro-LGBTQ policies and attitudes, Cape Town is a bastion of queer openness and tolerance. And while Johannesburg residents might scoff at the international popularity of Cape Town, saying it's too European and not a true African city, Cape Town residents don't really care. Instead, they're busy frolicking around their mountainous beach paradise, being as gay as possible.

But how has Cape Town developed this glowingly queer-affirmative identity? Some say it's the seaside location and the natural spirit of freedom that comes with the geography (sounds romantic!); others say it's because of international tourism and its influences. At this point, it almost doesn't matter. Cape Town is one of the most unexpected and visually stunning cities a queer traveler can add to their African itinerary.

Lindsay Louis, CEO of the Kirvan Fortuin Foundation

Lindsay Louis, an out-and-proud government official and former cultural attaché for South Africa, is now CEO of the Kirvan Fortuin Foundation, which uses dance to educate and create social awareness. The foundation focuses its work on marginalized areas of South Africa. Lindsay took over from the company's founder, dancer and choreographer Kirvan Fortuin, after his death in 2020.

Sassy Planet: What was it like growing up gay in South Africa? And what's your role in the community now?

Lindsay Louis: I never really had a challenge with my sexuality. It was always part of me. Even at school I always assumed leadership positions, and kids always voted for me. I never faced that type of homophobia at school. I was also protected at home. I am mixed race, and mixed-race South Africans can be very socially conservative— but they can be very open-minded when it comes to gay men, especially effeminate gay men, who of course are your dressmakers, hairdressers, and so on. So gay people have always been visible in my community.

Now, I'm the CEO of the Kirvan Fortuin Foundation. We do projects concerning human rights. Kirvan was an internationally renowned dancer. He started the first ballroom house in South Africa, the House of Le Cap. He saw dance as a tool for social change. I took over the organization after he was brutally murdered in June 2020. His death is being investigated as a possible hate crime.

SP: Many African gays see Cape Town as the continent's queer capital. Can you say more about that?

LL: Cape Town has always been the most liberal city in South Africa, even during apartheid days. We have a lot of gay people. People tend to feel much freer here. But homophobia does exist here, and people can still be subjected to hate speech and hate crimes. In Cape Town there's even a tradition of hosting gay beauty pageants. Sometimes these pageants take place in straight clubs, and it's widely accepted.

SP: Why is South Africa so much more progressive in terms of LGBTQ rights than its African neighbors?

LL: You can't really compare South Africa to other countries in Africa; our history is totally different. That's because of apartheid, and because of the highly industrialized nature of this country. And also because gay people had a role in the fight for freedom in this country. Simon Nkoli [1957–1998] was the father of the gay rights movement in South Africa. The people who fought for freedom fought to have the African National Congress build LGBT rights into the human rights of the new constitution. And even though we were oppressed under apartheid, there was tolerance. We were there, we said we were there, and we were quite vocal about it.

(1)

1 & 2: A House of Le Cap Vogue Ball.

(2)

Top Cape Town
To-Dos for Ho-Mos

Robben Island

The former prison island where Nelson Mandela was jailed for 18 years; now a UNESCO World Heritage Site.

Table Mountain

One of the most popular tourist sites of South Africa, a picturesque flat mountain overlooking Cape Town.

Sandy Bay beach

Pristine nudist beach where gays like to sunbathe and relax; difficult to access but worth the trek.

District Six Museum

Museum dedicated to District Six, a neighborhood whose culture was destroyed by means of forced resident removals under the system of apartheid.

Aquila Game Reserve

A popular place to go on safari as a day trip from Cape Town.

Johannesburg, South Africa

To really experience South Africa, you have to visit its biggest, most chaotic, and most diverse city: Johannesburg. Some might say Cape Town is to San Francisco as Johannesburg is to New York. Where Cape Town is picturesque, Johannesburg is maybe a bit less so. Where Cape Town is walkable, Johannesburg is massive and spreads out in all directions. Where Cape Town is laid back, Johannesburg is energized and ready to party. Where Cape Town has campy, fun drag queens, Johannesburg has mean, bitchy ones (… okay, that last part probably isn't true, we just figured we'd see how far the comparisons could go).

Originally established as a gold mining outpost, Johannesburg made international headlines throughout the latter half of the twentieth century as international condemnation of South Africa's racial segregation policies boiled over.

Its Soweto municipality was the site of a famous uprising in 1976 which made apartheid front-page news worldwide. Since the complete overhaul of its government and the dismantling of apartheid in the early 1990s, South Africa has made leaps and gains in the direction of racial and LGBTQ equality—but there is still much work to be done.

Voguing the House Down with Nicholas Lawrence

Nicholas Lawrence is a radio presenter based in Johannesburg. He is also the mother of the up-and-coming vogue ball group House of Helianthus.

Sassy Planet: Tell us about yourself, and what it's like to be queer in Johannesburg.
Nicholas Lawrence: I grew up and have spent all my life in Johannesburg. I'm a radio presenter. Personally, I stepped into the queer scene really late, around the age of 25. That's like 50 in gay years.

With South Africa having one of the most progressive constitutions in the world for queer people, you'd think it would mostly be rainbows, glitter, and feathers. Johannesburg is definitely one of the more accepting cities in South Africa— the culture for queer people is really breathtaking—but with its drawbacks, of course. Could queers have more visibility? Yes. I've seen it evolve, and [seen] a lot more cis-het people becoming more open to queer people and spaces, but there's definitely still a way to go. I can't not mention the pushback and abuse queer people still encounter in this country. It isn't *all* rainbows all the time.

I think Johannesburg is unique in that there are so many cultures, genders, sexual identities, and different types of people, styles, and openness to expression. Jo'burg is *really* fast-paced. It's known as the City of Gold, and is also (fun fact!) the largest city in the world not built on a coastline, river, or lake.

With the growth and visibility of ball culture making a come-back (don't think it left; it just died down a bit), we're seeing a new wave of queer collectives. We also see movements for inclusion and visibility, with queer event organizations like Le Grand Ball and Vogue Nights Jozi. The scene itself is very small but growing, and I enjoy being part of the activism—cattiness included.

That being said, Black South Africans have experienced a lot

The children of the House of Helianthus at Le Grand Ball, including Nicholas Lawrence on the right.

of transphobia, to the point of murder within rural South Africa, and white queers of South Africa aren't able to resonate with or understand the complexities of these issues. As a mixed-race person it's easy to see the separate issues.

SP: A complex situation for sure. In terms of the more joyous side of being queer in the city, what LGBTQ events would you recommend?
NL: I'd definitely say Johannesburg Pride. It genuinely depends on the vibe one is looking for. The best party is Pussy Party, an event hosted on Thursdays by Vogue Nights. You can come across literally everything there but an alien.

Alternatively, a club called Babylon. The entire Braamfontein [neighborhood's] nightlife is great for queer spaces. Everyone is just out to have a great time.

Nicholas Lawrence's
Top Jo'burg To-Dos for Ho-Mos

The Apartheid Museum

"For me, being an activist, and our history being as rich as it is, this museum is a must."

Rhino and Lion Nature Reserve

"I've only been there once, but, this being Africa and all, you have to see a big cat."

Vilakazi Street in Soweto

"For food, atmosphere, and nightlife."

Maboneng Precinct

"And specifically The Living Room, a speakeasy with the best vibe I know."

Le Grand Ball

"Attend a Le Grand Ball if you're lucky enough to be in town at the right time, as they don't happen very often."

Le Grand Ball:

Le Grand Ball is one of Johannesburg's premier events for gender nonconforming, queer, trans, and drag performers. Led by Mother of The Ball Treyvone Moo, these productions incorporate African music and culture into a unique vogue ball experience that continually reshapes the ballroom scene.

(1)

(2)

1: Khotso Rams and Tsepo Kgatlhane at
Le Grand's Fetish Ball. 2 & next spread:
The House of Queer Mafia at Le Grand Ball.

Lagos, Nigeria

L agos is one of the 20 largest cities in the world and home to a thriving fashion scene, internationally renowned artists, mega pop stars who work with the likes of Beyoncé, a film hub called Nollywood that produces over 1,000 movies a year, and even beach resorts (including one named Moist!). At the same time, Nigeria notoriously enforces anti-homosexuality laws, thus pushing its queer scene deeper underground. In recent years, the government has been aggressive in arresting large numbers of people at private events and charging them with crimes.

Telling Their Own Stories: Harry Itie's *Rustin Times*

In July 2017, journalist Harry Itie started the online publication the *Rustin Times* to reframe how stories about the Nigerian LGBTQ community are presented. His platform showcases film, art, and music and also discusses community issues via op-ed pieces and interviews. The site was named after queer civil rights activist Bayard Rustin, who worked alongside Martin Luther King, Jr. In the 1960s, Rustin was pushed out of the public spotlight by many civil rights leaders, who thought his sexuality and ties to communist organizations would hurt the movement.

Sassy Planet: What is Lagos's reputation within Nigeria?
Harry Itie: A lot of people believe that when you come to Lagos, things are going to be better— that you will get opportunities. This is "where it's at." It's the entertainment and fashion hub for the country. Pop culture thrives in Lagos.

SP: Why did you start the *Rustin Times*?
HI: We noticed that the mainstream media wasn't doing a good job in talking about the issues that the LGBTQ community faces. The media wasn't being very ethical, and was coming to the issues with a lot of bias. So it was important to create a platform that would be balanced, and be able to talk about the issues in ways that will be better for the community. That will not promote violence.

SP: How did you select the publication's name?
HI: Bayard Rustin was a queer Black man. Because of that, he was erased from the history of the civil rights movement. I think for Africans, especially the ones who live on the continent, that is what we face. The constant hiding of yourself, and the way that news of your sexuality comes up—that's all people see. All the hard work, and everything you have done over time, becomes irrelevant. So it was our way of honoring Bayard's life and the work he did.

SP: What kinds of stories do you like to tell?
HI: We are an alternative news platform, so any information you would get from the mainstream, you can get on this platform. We tell stories from a queer perspective. When mainstream media is vilifying an issue that has to do with queer people, we will

not do that. We'll do it in a much more balanced way.

SP: What's most exciting about the queer community in Lagos?
HI: The filmmaking. We have well-told, nuanced queer stories. There is *ÌFÈ* [a 2020 film about a lesbian couple], which took everybody by storm. We did a series of interviews with the producers and the actors. To see women loving themselves on film is a big deal in the Nigerian film industry. We are slowly making a mark. Everything is underground, but we're trying to figure out how to balance that and be safe in a country with anti-gay laws.

SP: What is the state of queer activism currently?
HI: The movement is becoming more active. We are [involved on] all fronts: pop culture, media, politics, lobbying, and litigation. Organizations are springing up in different areas. We need stronger alliances with the global queer community, and [to] realize that we all win together.

SP: What's exciting about Lagos?
HI: People are realizing that there is a vibrant culture. Our music is our biggest export. Our artists are doing great on an international stage. In Beyoncé's film *Black is King* you have WizKid, Tiwa Savage, Burna Boy—they all became popular in Lagos.

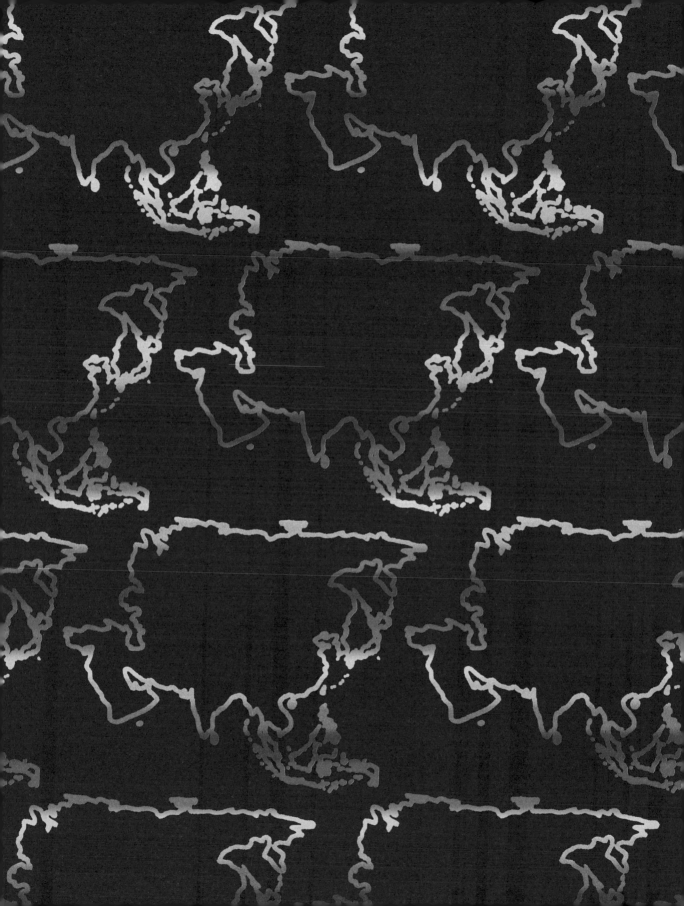

Amman, Jordan

Jordan doesn't criminalize LGBTQ identities, and trans people can even have their gender marker modified here—but locals say that being openly queer nonetheless carries a huge social stigma in Amman and across the country. Still, homosexuality has been decriminalized in Jordan for consenting people over the age of 16 since 1951. England only partially decriminalized it in 1967, whereas the United States waited until 2003 to get its act together. While Amman has few queer spaces (and many of the visible venues are dominated by the city's large expat community and tourists), the scene is nonetheless very present, a situation unlike in many neighboring countries, where it has been forced underground.

A Queer Platform for the Middle East: *My.Kali*

My.Kali is a website and online magazine (or "webzine," if you will) covering the Middle East and North Africa. It was established in 2007 by a group of artists, students, and political activists interested in addressing local social problems. The magazine covers a wide range of topics, including women's rights, LGBTQ issues, freedom of speech, and more.

Sassy Planet: Tell us about *My.Kali*.
My.Kali: My.Kali magazine is a conceptual queer and feminist magazine that publishes on matters related to social issues, queerness, the alternative and underground art and music scenes, gender, sex and sexuality, identity, and orientation. *My.Kali* serves as a platform and as an alternative form of activism. It reflects unheard marginalized opinions, uncensored voices, and unabashed attitudes. The publication thrives on local and regional pop culture and the underground scene, using its platform to present new artistic and political concepts.

   My.Kali builds on the understanding that cultural stereotypes stem from countless factors and discourses that are created and reinforced every day. It addresses these stereotypes through visually engaging features and social commentary with a local and regional flavor. We aim

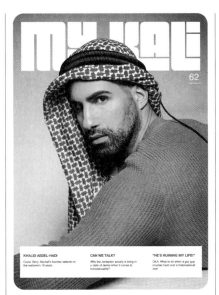

A *My.Kali* magazine cover featuring its founder Khalid "Kali" Abdel-Hadi.

to demonstrate diversity and fight repressive forms and norms with art therapy, photography, and visual innovation. *My.Kali* is built by many bloggers, emerging and established writers, experimental photographers, and independent designers and artists, who come

together from across the Middle East and North Africa (MENA) and the diaspora to put together empowering and informative editorial.

SP: How did *My.Kali* start? And where are your readers from?
M.K: My.Kali was started in 2007 by a young Jordanian/Palestinian student named Khalid Abdel-Hadi, who serves as its editor in chief and creative director. The magazine started due to the lack of both online queer Arab resources and inclusive media and platforms. *My.Kali* readers stem from all across the MENA region and diaspora.

SP: A lot of LGBTQ people think of Tel Aviv or Beirut when they think of a gay center in the Middle East. Where do you think Amman fits into this list of gay destinations?
M.K: We try as much as possible not to compare, as we work across the MENA region and each

country's status is different than the next. We wouldn't promote it as a gay destination, but rather as an amazing destination in general. Amman specifically could be categorized as a gentrified dream, with interesting cafés and bars in secret little corners.

SP: Amman seems surprisingly tolerant and open toward queer people. Is there an explanation for this?

M.K: Amman, the country's capital, is relatively accepting of LGB people—or at least, middle-class, wealthy, educated queers who pass. Yet trans people, working-class queers, those outside the capital, and anyone presenting as queer in public still face severe repression. In the context of Jordan's uneven political climate, systemic queerphobia in the rest of the Middle East, and international queer movements that center whiteness, demonize Islam, and treat Middle Eastern queers as either victims or primitives, liberating queer communities is a minefield—one that regularly claims lives. We believe that a huge part of the tolerance here comes from the hard work of our activist community, including our work to establish a healthy visibility and conversation when discussing LGBT+ matters.

SP: Do you have any interesting stories, myths, or history to share about LGBTQ Amman?

M.K: A gay-friendly bar called RGB (which quickly got a reputation as a gay bar) closed after the owner received a message threatening that if it didn't shut down, "all its customers will be put in solitary cells." Another club with an "LGBT following" called Fab was noted late in 2008 to have been opening and closing unpredictably, also reportedly due to threats. These establishments both opened in 2007 and were allegedly the first such establishments to offer an environment in which some LGBT Jordanians were willing to be seen together in public.

Top Queer-Friendly Amman Establishments

✿ Jabal al-Weibdeh, Jabal Amman, and downtown Amman are some of the most friendly areas.

✿ Joz Hind restaurant.

✿ Shams el Balad, a restaurant, grocery store, and design shop.

✿ Maestro bar and restaurant, for music and concerts.

✿ Café de Paris.

✿ Copas Central, for Latin-inspired cuisine.

✿ Dali bar.

✿ Turtle Green Tea Bar.

✿ The Corner's Pub, for music and concerts.

My.Kali's
Top Things to See and Do in Amman and Jordan

The fundamentals

"While in Jordan, see the Dead Sea, Petra, and Wadi Rum."

Downtown Amman

"Walk in the souks, buying all sorts of spices and souvenirs; and eat *kunafah* at Habibah, hummus and falafel at Hashem, and *mansaf* (Jordan's national dish) at Al Quds."

The "Friday Market"

"Also known as Souk el-Joumea. It's a large secondhand clothing market located on the edge of downtown. The market is vast so if you want to make it all the way around, you may want to set aside at least half a day. If you have a keen eye you'll find a few gems every time you visit, from PVC pants and '90s Calvin Klein jeans to early 2000s army fatigues, parkas, wedding dresses, and everything in between! A lot of the fashions in our shoots come from there; our stylists live for it."

Rumi Café's terrace

"We recommend having a coffee here. The cardamom cakes and Iraqi teas are to die for."

Namliyeh

"Make sure to visit this shop for artisan jams, botanical teas, and raw honey. Their slogan is: 'We design food experiences inspired by the landscape.'"

CLSTR

"A seasonal underground club. Their dancefloor is inclusive and friendly."

Bangkok, Thailand

W ith its English name combining euphemisms for "sex" and "penis," it should perhaps come as no surprise that Bangkok has long been a haven for queers in Thailand and throughout Southeast Asia. Visitors flock to the city to take part in its vibrant LGBTQ culture, which is growing and evolving each year.

Bangkok's gay scene is mostly associated with massive circuit parties, several of which take place each April during Thailand's Songkran water festival, when the entire country turns into one gigantic water fight. Though the revelry is nationwide, the gays (never ones to miss out on an opportunity to throw a wet T-shirt contest) have turned the festival into one of the biggest queer celebrations in Asia. GCIRCUIT Songkran, a circuit party that coincides with the festival, attracts 20,000 of the world's muscled masses for three days of pool parties, drag performances, and gold lamé booty shorts.

Circuit parties, understandably, aren't everyone's jam. Fortunately, there is something in Bangkok for every shade of queer. The Silom neighborhood is the best-known hub for nightlife, bars, and drag performances. On a typical night, locals and tourists alike drink and eat in one of the many LGBTQ bars along Silom Soi 4 early in the evening. Just across the street, on Silom Soi 2, clubs are packed with queers dancing the night away.

Trasher, Ark Saroj's Anti-Circuit Party

Ark Saroj is a photographer and party promoter based in Bangkok. He co-founded Trasher, one of the city's biggest alternative LGBTQ parties, back in 2007 to help counter the dominant circuit party vibe that he felt had taken over Bangkok and much of Southeast Asia. In recent years he's also become a photographer, documenting much of the queer scene in the city. Saroj explains that Trasher is meant to provide a space for alternative queers interested in a different type of scene. Different how? "Our music has words," he says.

Sassy Planet: Describe Trasher and why you decided to start it.
Ark Saroj: We started the party back in 2007 so we could listen to the type of music we wanted— old music from the 1990s like Britney, NSYNC, and Backstreet Boys. We called the party Trasher because it's trash music, but we loved it, and you couldn't hear that music anywhere. The gay scene then was mostly at huge circuit parties.

At first it was just like 50 people from our university who would show up and dance. But it started growing in 2012 when we started doing videos to help promote the party and they'd go viral. We did a famous one after a huge flood in Bangkok left the city deserted. We dressed up my friend like Adele and did a parody, with him walking around the empty streets doing bad lip-synching to "Hello." Now, the party is huge. It happens in big dance clubs and 3,500 people show up. The music is different now, though—now that the '90s are

(1)

stigmatized. In the Buddhist world, if you're gay or trans, they believe you did something bad in a past life. You have bad karma. They have sympathy for you, but it's pity. Life for gay people is very easy in Thailand, especially compared to other places in Asia, but you won't see an openly gay politician with a good position in parliament. You won't see openly gay governors of Bangkok. You won't see a CEO of a company come out as gay. This is why we don't have Pride here—no one wants to associate their brand with gay culture. Maybe in 20 years, but not now.

hip again you can hear that music everywhere. So mostly it's now super millennial pop music that's current.

SP: How does Trasher compare to other gay nightlife events in Bangkok?
AS: It was unique when Trasher started, but now the scene has become mainstream. This kind of party happens at lots of gay bars now, with Trasher music. Just add in some drag queens. That's been our influence on the scene here.

Drag is a big deal in a lot of nightlife in Bangkok too. We had a *Drag Race Thailand* for two seasons, which helped make it more popular. But it's different here because most of the people who do drag in the West are cisgender. In Bangkok, it's mostly trans performers. It's hard to find a boy drag queen here. This is different from the "ladyboy" shows, which are mostly for tourists. Those are huge productions with lots of costume changes. It's extravagant and over-the-top. But it's done before a mostly straight audience, who sit and watch it like any other cultural show. The shows that happen in places like The Stranger Bar are real drag shows and have become famous here for both tourists and locals.

SP: How has Bangkok's queer scene changed in recent years?
AS: It's more accepting now, but in an annoying way. Everyone here just wants to find a husband. Back then, in the old days, it was harder, but I think the structure of society also taught gay men to be strong; to know what we want and stand up for ourselves. Now, everyone is just looking for daddies. They want to find a wealthy middle-class husband and get married in Taiwan or the UK.

LGBTQ people aren't discriminated against as much anymore, but we're still

(2)

1-4: Trasher events. The party provides a fresh, alternative option for Bangkok's queer revelers.

(3)

(4)

BY THE NUMBERS

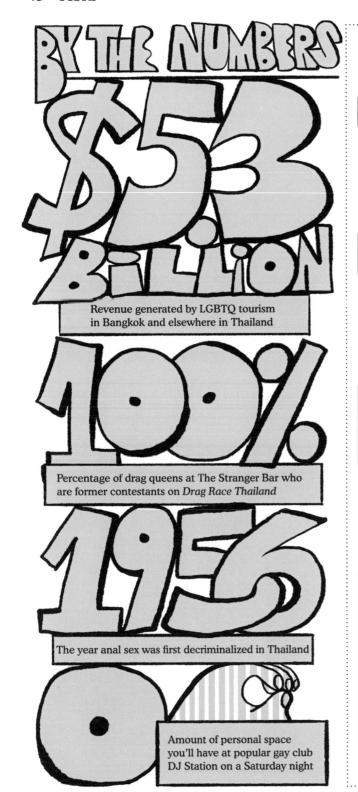

$5.3 BILLION

Revenue generated by LGBTQ tourism in Bangkok and elsewhere in Thailand

100%

Percentage of drag queens at The Stranger Bar who are former contestants on *Drag Race Thailand*

1956

The year anal sex was first decriminalized in Thailand

0

Amount of personal space you'll have at popular gay club DJ Station on a Saturday night

Chat WITH A LOCAL

MochaGreenTea: Have you tried the saunas in Bangkok?

Sassy_Planet: No, what are they like?

MochaGreenTea: They're much nicer than the ones in Europe. Really clean. They're popular; some have good parties.

Sassy_Planet: Which ones are the most popular?

MochaGreenTea: Sauna Mania is my favorite. It's mostly locals, but some tourists come too. At Babylon you'll see lots of tourists. It's also a hotel, so they have a really nice pool that's great for hot days.

Sassy_Planet: And the saunas throw parties?

MochaGreenTea: Babylon throws a lot of parties. I went to a foam party there recently. They pumped all this foam into parts of the maze, and it was packed. Everyone was dancing and having a good time. But I mostly like to just hang out at the pool there. It's easy to talk and meet people there. A good place to go with friends. You can hang out and drink and chat and laugh, and then excuse yourself when you want to take a visit to the backrooms. It just doesn't feel as gross as the saunas I've been to in Berlin or Paris.

Ark Saroj's
Top Bangkok To-Dos
for Ho-Mos

Trasher

"Of course. The scene is mostly queer,
and definitely not for people who like
circuit parties."

Go Grrrls

"A fun queer party that lots of lesbians and
queers are going to. But again, not for circuit
queens. They wouldn't like it."

The Stranger Bar

"It's the best for drag. Very touristy,
but still my favorite bar in Bangkok."

Ho Chi Minh City, Vietnam

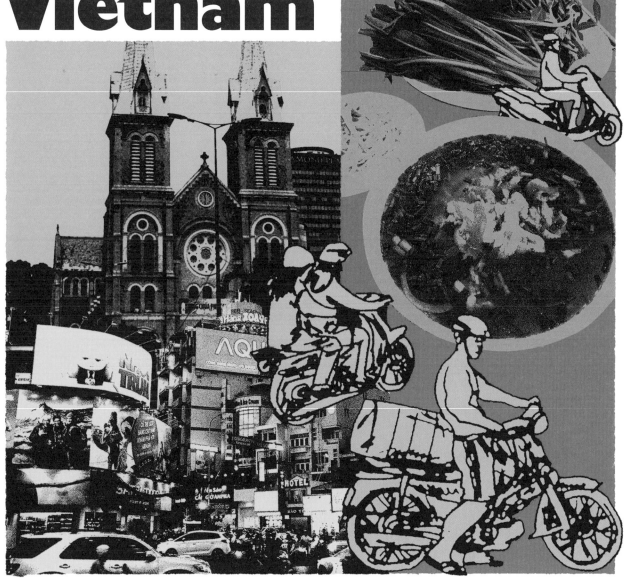

If all of Asia were smooshed into a single metropolis, Ho Chi Minh City would be the "up-and-coming" neighborhood, soon to be rebranded by real estate agents. Over the last decade much has been said about the economic development and rising business profile here,

which has caught the attention of the West—including luxury travel outlets that spill the tea on the "undiscovered" charm of the city. On the apps, where people list their location as "HCMC" or "Saigon," the grid is filled with a mix of international tourists and locals. And with numerous men-only saunas bearing names like Thé SixtyNine Zone or 3 Some Spa, there is a blatant attempt to attract Western gay travelers.

Many of Ho Chi Minh City's queer establishments are expat-owned and cater to the tourists, with Top 40 music and weekend drag revues. The gay venues are found on De Tham street in District 1, which is referred to as the backpacker area. There are also monthly queer parties, including Full Disclosure and GenderFunk. LGBTQ locals tend to frequent coffee shops, where they can sip boba tea or sing karaoke.

Mixing Gender with Funk

GenderFunk is a party based in Ho Chi Minh City that provides a space for the city's queer population to express their sexuality and identity however they damn well please. "You. Do. You." as the group says on its social media pages.

Sassy Planet: What's the queer scene in Ho Chi Minh City like?
GenderFunk: HCMC doesn't have that many gay bars per se. However, it does have a growing queer scene, with some of the best drag in Asia. The queer scene is very party-centric, but there are also many queer evenings at straight bars and quizzes, and other places. There were more queer bars in the past, but many have closed down.

The scene is growing, with lots of queer people moving here due to the relaxed attitude toward gay people. Notable gay bars are Republic, The Tipsy Unicorn, Whiskey & Wares (all on De Tham street), Haus of Royalty (on Cong Quynh), and Twist Coffee (on Thao Dien).

SP: Describe your party.
GF: GenderFunk is an inclusive space for all people to express

A GenderFunk party.

(1)

[their] gender and sexuality. It started as a bunch of expats and local Vietnamese people combining to create a community of artists who do various events, from runway battles and drag shows to exhibitions and other craziness. Born from a desire to have a stage for the freaks who never get booked, our stage is now a platform for the new generation of queer artists.

SP: What about meeting guys and cruising?
GF: The hookup scene is rife here. Grindr is packed, and there are several saunas and hookup spas for decent prices.

SP: What's the general attitude toward queer tourists?
GF: Gay tourism here is great, with many cool places to see and visit, and some very gay-friendly hotels and restaurants. Kissing and public affection is uncommon for all Vietnamese people, so being discreet isn't just for queer people. However, Vietnamese society is accepting of queer people, and there is no aggression toward them. Within the families of Vietnamese people, there are difficulties of course.

(2)

(3)

Chat WITH A LOCAL

Sassy_Planet: What's the gay scene like in HCMC?

VietGuy: It's a small scene, but pretty friendly and active. There's a group called GenderFunk that puts on events and parties.

Sassy_Planet: What's a normal weekend there like?

VietGuy: There aren't many gay bars, but the nightlife is pretty mixed. I hang out at cocktail bars mostly, and then occasionally late parties at music venues. The scene is very house and techno.

Sassy_Planet: Is it easy to meet people out, or do most people connect online?

VietGuy: It is easy to meet out, but the apps definitely help people connect.

Sassy_Planet: What makes HCMC cooler than other Asian cities?

VietGuy: The charm—from the people to the food, and overall the ease of life. It's cool to watch this place develop. It has a very entrepreneurial energy.

1-3: GenderFunk parties.

Jeddah, Saudi Arabia

حدة غير

A port city nestled on the coast of the Red Sea, Jeddah is best known as the gateway to Mecca for the millions of people who travel to Saudi Arabia annually for the Hajj. One of the bigger cities in the country, it has markets and architecture dating back to the seventh century, when it was an important trade port, but also explosive wealth that has brought in skyscrapers and hypermodern technologies. Jeddah has a reputation for being the most open region in a country with an absolute monarchy. Despite harsh penalties for breaking laws, a vibrant gay world unfolds behind the closed doors of high-rise apartments, embassies, beachfront villas, and highly secured compounds.

Chat WITH A ~~LOCAL~~ VISITING RESEARCHER

Sassy_Planet: What makes Jeddah different?

Mo: A common phrase (if not cliché) uttered by Jeddawis is *Jeddah Ghair*, or "Jeddah is Different." It refers to the deep histories of Red Sea cosmopolitanism that made this place economically, culturally, and politically exceptional to the larger enveloping fold of the Saudi national state. The phrase has become something of a regional branding device used by telecommunication companies: "Summers in Jeddah are different." There's a mall in town called Ana Ghair Mall, or "I'm Different Mall." But I've often heard the phrase uttered by friends at queer or other wildly liberal scenes unfolding in micro-villas of north Jeddah—like a wild house party that played Eliad Cohen mixes all night. Being different is now an attempt at globally recognizable sameness.

Sassy_Planet: What's the nightlife scene like there?

Mo: In Jeddah, you stay out very late on Thursday nights and into Friday morning. It's often the case that parties are just getting started at 3am. On Fridays, everything is closed until late afternoon for prayers. By 10am, the apps are full of headless torsos looking to hook up.

Sassy_Planet: What's the gay app scene like in Jeddah?

Mo: On the apps, a common greeting in Arabic is *mumkin nta'aref*, or "maybe we can get to know each other." I've always loved the tentative and vague sweetness of the phrase. But an important part of this courtship is knowledge of whether or not one is "foreign" or "local." This is the sort of place where those categories are not plainly apparent. On the apps, people would ask me, "Are you sure you're not Saudi? You look very Saudi." Or, "I think you're Syrian but don't want to say."

Sassy_Planet: Is it easy for foreigners to meet other LGBTQ people on the apps?

Mo: Many of my Saudi friends tell me they prefer talking to foreigners—that it feels safer; more anonymous. Foreigners often have material access, like hotel rooms and private apartments, which matters. But as with everything it depends on what kind of foreigner you are. A lot of the profiles say, "Chat in English only, no Arabic." Others say, "No Pakistanis. No Filipinos." But chat on the apps only lasts so long before they move to other more ephemeral or unmonitored applications, like Snapchat or BlackBerry Messenger.

An underground party in Jeddah.

Mumbai, India

Many consider Mumbai (or Bombay, as many of the locals still call it) to be the queer center of India. The city perhaps deserves that title simply for being the birthplace of Bollywood, the famed Hindi-language film industry. Mumbai has long been home to many queer bars and clubs, but when homosexuality was illegal here, these spaces largely operated underground. Since the decriminalization of same-sex relations in 2018, however, that has all started to change. Many LGBTQ establishments are now out and proud, making it much easier for travelers to find and connect with the local scene.

Ankit Bhuptani: Leading the Way to a More Inclusive Hinduism

Ankit Bhuptani is the founder of the Queer Hindu Alliance. The Mumbai-based advocacy and support group promotes a more inclusive version of Hinduism by creating safe spaces for LGBTQ Hindus and allies to engage, share, and support each other without fear or discrimination.

Sassy Planet: Describe the organization you started.

Ankit Bhuptani: The Queer Hindu Alliance connects the dots between sexuality and spirituality. We're a support group that helps people when they come out, and helps answer questions from people's families about religion and sexuality. We're also the voice for queer Hindus as a community. And we're an advocacy group.

SP: Homosexuality was decriminalized in India in 2018. How has that impacted the LGBTQ community in Mumbai and around the country?

AB: The Indian queer community has seen such a dramatic change within my lifetime. I was born in 1992. We've seen more progress than any other generation. The recent ruling by the Supreme Court decriminalizing homosexuality is just the latest development. Everyone was waiting for it to happen. And society was really ready to come out and support it. During the last few Prides in Mumbai, we've seen so many organizations and corporations come out in support. We have parent groups, doctors' groups, teachers' groups, even a cats and dogs lovers' association.

SP: How has Pride changed in Mumbai over the years?

AB: I've worked on our Pride organizing committee for the past nine years. Back when I first started, we would hand out these free face masks to people who wanted to attend Pride but who weren't out yet or didn't want to be identified. So much has changed in terms of acceptance that we don't even feel the need to do that anymore. Lots of smaller towns in India are also doing their own Prides now. We've seen so much change at such a fast pace—so much positivity and acceptance. But in the same way that so many more people are coming out of the closet, the haters are coming

A Queer Hindu Alliance event.

(1)

out of the closet too. So that is definitely a concern for us.

SP: What has the impact been on gay bars, clubs, and businesses since homosexuality was decriminalized?
AB: I was recently on a panel about the economy in South Asia, and we discussed "pink money," the contributions of LGBTQIA businesses to the economy. We found that 6 percent of India's GDP is part of the pink economy. And that's growing—queer businesses and bars are now out in the open. Mumbai doesn't have a dedicated gay bar, but now we have multiple gay parties

happening every week. These parties are out and proud and posting on social media. They're part of the mainstream in a good way.

SP: In 2020, even Bollywood came out, with its first movie featuring a gay romance!
AB: That was *Shubh Mangal Zyada Saavdhan*. Something you should know about India is that, whenever someone does something, we always like to say it's the first without checking the history. We've had plenty of queer characters in television and film. This might be the first to do such a big romantic storyline,

but it's not the first. Mumbai is also home to South Asia's largest queer film festival, called KASHISH Mumbai International Queer Film Festival. (Well, at least they say they are the largest; I would probably fact-check that!) So, lots of queer movies and characters are included in that.

1: Mumbai Pride. 2: A Queer Azaadi Mumbai event.

Queer Azaadi Mumbai

Queer Azaadi Mumbai (QAM) is a collective of individuals and organizations that voluntarily come together with the aim of securing human rights for queer individuals in India. "Our mission is to ensure that every individual gets to enjoy equal rights in India; that is what our constitution promises us," explains Saurabh B., one of the organizers of Mumbai's annual Pride celebrations. "It goes without saying that fighting discrimination and violence is our inherent duty."

QAM also organizes Mumbai's Pride events, which are the biggest in the country. "Although Kolkata did the first Pride march back in the 1990s, that wasn't followed by much activity," says Saurabh. "Hence, Mumbai Pride has kind of achieved a pioneer status. We've seen crowds of more than 8,000 individuals."

However, QAM's events are not just centered around parades and celebrations. The group also organizes protests, solidarity gatherings, panel discussions and more to debate and shine light on issues impacting the local queer community. "The goal here is to reiterate that queer individuals are very much a part of society, and we deliver our social responsibility in the right spirit," Saurabh says. QAM also supports at least one non-queer cause

(2)

every year, like beach cleaning activities after public festivals, donating funds to victims of famine, and, most recently, organizing mutual aid efforts.

"In Mumbai, you are sure to find something that's of interest to you. Due to our multiethnic culture, every individual gets served something to their taste," Saurabh says. "Living and food costs here are quite high, but traveling can be quite cheap, and exploring the city couldn't be easier due to its well-developed infrastructure and superb public transport."

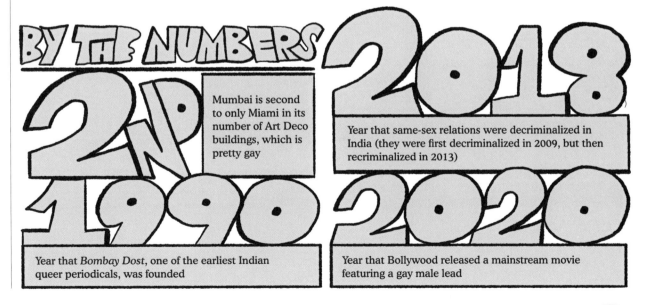

BY THE NUMBERS

2ND Mumbai is second to only Miami in its number of Art Deco buildings, which is pretty gay

2018 Year that same-sex relations were decriminalized in India (they were first decriminalized in 2009, but then recriminalized in 2013)

1990 Year that *Bombay Dost*, one of the earliest Indian queer periodicals, was founded

2020 Year that Bollywood released a mainstream movie featuring a gay male lead

Mumbai's "First Drag King," Durga Gawde

Durga Gawde, aka Shakti, is a sculptor, performer, and drag artist from Mumbai. They seamlessly incorporate all three types of art into their work and are on a mission to blend the gender binary in India in a way they haven't seen done before.

Sassy Planet: What was it like growing up in Mumbai?
Durga Gawde: For a bit of context, in India it's illegal to identify the sex of a fetus, because infanticide is a big problem [as are sex-selective abortions, due to a bias toward male children]. People here don't support people with a womb. Arranged marriage is still part of our culture, as is the dowry system. There is a movement to abolish these practices, but they are deeply ingrained. I grew up with a dad who was an artist

and a mom who worked as an administrator. So I was always surrounded by artists and strange people, but it was still pretty homophobic. My parents still made sure to say, "That's them, this is us. We're not connected to any of that."

SP: How long have you been performing and making art?
DG: I studied sculpture at the Rhode Island School of Design (RISD). It was my dream school, and I got in. It was amazing. It was also the first time I'd spent time with trans people outside of the context I grew up in. Here, we all know trans kids in India, but we just don't talk about it. But there, it was my first time really understanding gender. After RISD, I came back to India to teach design at the Indian School of Design and Innovation in Bombay. I felt suffocated, after my time at RISD, being put back into this Indian female box. I wanted to do activism and be comfortable being a genderfluid person.

SP: How did that impact your artwork and activism?
DG: I wanted my art to be about my activism, but I wasn't ready to release my identity publicly yet. I waited for several years after moving back, and then I became all about creating queer

representation full force—photo shoots, editorials, interviews. I performed for a designer at Lakme Fashion Week, one of the biggest fashion events in India, in a show called Gender Bender. I was in a bathtub basically having a suggestive orgy with all these people in really fancy clothes. These are the things I used to do at RISD for fun. Once I was back in my country, I didn't feel like I could show this to friends and family. But then I decided, fuck it, I'm going to be here and be me. Because if I'm not me in my own country, how am I being the person I needed to see when I was a kid?

SP: How did you get into doing drag?
DG: The last three or four years of my activism brought me into connection to drag and drag culture. I didn't even know we had such a big drag culture in India. I met my drag mom, Rani KoHEnur, who is like the queen of drag in Mumbai, one night at the Kitty Su Mumbai [nightclub]. Alaska Thunderfuck was performing. She put her hand in her bra at one point and took out a condom that said "Triple X" on it, threw it in my face, and said, "Take that, bitch!" It was amazing, and I went backstage after to meet her and Rani. I showed them a picture of me when

I had put on a five o'clock shadow with some makeup. My entire posture changed. I looked like a total fuckboy. I showed it to them and they were both like, "Wait, what do you do?" I said I was a sculptor, and they were like, "What the fuck are you doing? You need to be doing drag."

Rani took me under her wing at that point, and suddenly I had this world open up for me. She said, "I'm going to train you and

SP: You call yourself "India's first drag king." Are there not many other drag kings in India?
DG: I don't know of anybody else before me doing the type of drag I do as a drag king. But drag culture happens in many different ways in India. There are different performers in different languages, even in different tribes. But they don't refer to themselves or what they're doing as drag. It's more in the realm of theater, so it's not so

the word that remains is Shakti—we use it to refer to feminine energy. The strongest energy in Indian culture isn't masculine energy, it's feminine. So that's where I got Shakti—it's "Durga" without the gender.

SP: How do you see your activism, drag, and sculpture all working together?
DG: I look at my life like a flower. The middle is my essence. But then I do whatever the fuck I want to, as long as I keep coming back to what's important to me—my essence.

Before I had my drag debut, I did a sculpture-performance piece that involved insane shapes and, like, ten thousand LED lights that changed color. I called it the *Rainbow Revolution*, which I use in my work as a hashtag. My activism, sculpture, and drag journey started there. I walked around in drag in a giant cape, talking to people about rainbows and what they meant to them. Those conversations were livestreamed into my installation, so you could hear what people were saying, but anonymously.

When I met Rani I started to do drag more intensely. But the bars and clubs aren't really my scene. I'm not so much of a lip-synch performer as a visual artist. What I really want to do, actually, is create or inspire existing spaces to do queer events, but without alcohol. Like a queer book reading or cooking class, or a queer swimming class. Really, just anything you can think of with the word "queer" in front of it.

Durga Gawde performs as a drag king using the name Shakti.

book you, but you have to learn about this world. This is a craft." So I followed her around for about six months, watching her do her makeup and wardrobe, and then she was like, "You're ready." Drag also helped me understand my relationship to my body, and being nonbinary and trans, and what that meant to me. I learned there's no right or wrong way to be what you want to be.

visible. There was a well-known play about drag kings [a few years ago] called *Gentlemen's Club*, but that was just actresses dressing up like drag kings. They were characters.

SP: What does your drag name mean?
DG: Shakti is my drag name. "Durga" is the Hindu word for power. And actually, when you take out the gender from Durga,

Taipei, Taiwan

Taipei has become a progressive LGBTQ wonderland over the last decade, complete with muscle bears, saunas, a booming queer art scene, and the largest Pride event in East Asia. In addition to appointing trans woman Audrey Tang, a self-described "conservative anarchist," to its executive cabinet in 2016, Taiwan legalized same-sex marriage in 2019. For a time, Taipei was even home to an all-lesbian boy band called MISSTER.

The Ximen Red House area near the Ximending Night Market is Taipei's homo central, with more than 25 different queer bars, shops, and restaurants. The city has also become a hub for gay circuit parties like Mega Party, which takes place during the summer Dragon Boat Festival and attracts revelers from all over Taiwan and neighboring countries.

Wei-ming Temple

(1)

According to seventeenth-century folklore, the rabbit god Tu Shen is a Taoist deity that became known as the god of same-sex love (the word "rabbit" was a derogatory term for homosexuals in Chinese history).

The story tells of how a simple soldier, Hu Tianbao, had fallen in love with a higher-up imperial inspector. He was later caught spying on his crush through a bathroom wall and had to admit to having a boner. The inspector then had the soldier charged and sentenced to death. The horny dead soldier came back to haunt the dreams of a village elder, telling him that the gods of the underworld saw his crime as one of passion, and that they had anointed Hu Tianbao to be the rabbit god, Tu Shen, protector of the affairs of gay men. He then asked the elder to construct a shrine in his honor in Fujian province. By the eighteenth century, the temple had a cult following big enough to attract the ire of Qing dynasty officials, who saw the images of men embracing on its walls as immoral and tried to suppress the cult.

In 2006, Taoist priest Lu Wei-ming erected a temple to Tu Shen down a narrow alley in New Taipei. Now, almost 9,000 queer people visit the temple annually to seek celestial support in finding romance. The young priest claims that it is the world's only shrine currently dedicated to homosexual love. Wei-ming counsels worshipers in their hunt for soulmates by offering the rabbit god rice wine, or by noting prayers on a slip of paper that worshipers can sleep with under their pillows.

(2)

1: Priest Lu Wei-ming. 2: Offerings at the Wei-ming Temple.

Chat WITH A LOCAL

(1)

Sassy_Planet: Hi, Sugar_Ray, what do you do?

Sugar_Ray: I'm an engineer with a YouTube channel and an Instagram account. I like to take photos and videos of my gay friends.

Sassy_Planet: What do you love and recommend in Taipei?

Sugay_Ray: We have really nice food— try all the food! I recommend our hot springs [Taiwan has the highest concentration, as well as largest variety, of hot springs in the world]. Ximen Red House is the gay area; it's like the Castro of Taipei. And, the Taipei 101 building for shopping! Goldfish Bar is a nice place to drink and hang out with friends.

Sassy_Planet: How has the queer scene changed there over the years?

Sugar_Ray: Ten years ago we were a party city. Japanese, Korean, and Thai people came to Taiwan for the gay parade and big weekend parties—Taiwan is at the center of East Asia, making it easy to get here. But since government policies changed, there are fewer parties.

(2)

1: Taipei local Sugar Ray. 2: Ningxia Night Market.

Top Tapei
Tips for Bottoms

228 Peace Memorial Park

A park in the center of the old downtown that used to be a cruising area for gay men, and which was a featured location in the famous Taiwanese gay novel *Crystal Boys* (1983) by Pai Hsien-yung. It's now the site of a memorial to the February 28 massacre of Taiwanese people who rose up in 1947 to protest heavy-handed rule by the Kuomintang party.

Commander D

BDSM bar located in one of the oldest districts of Taipei.

Bars behind the Ximen Red House

Located behind the landmark Red House, a historic market building built in 1908 (during the Japanese colonial era) that's been restored as a cultural center, is a group of gay bars. The bars tend to get more bear-ish as you walk further around the back.

Aniki Spa

A bathhouse/sauna for the boys. It has high-tech entry using a swipe card and is very clean.

Fairy Taipei

This bistro in the East District of Taipei transforms into a cocktail bar later in the evening.

Tokyo, Japan

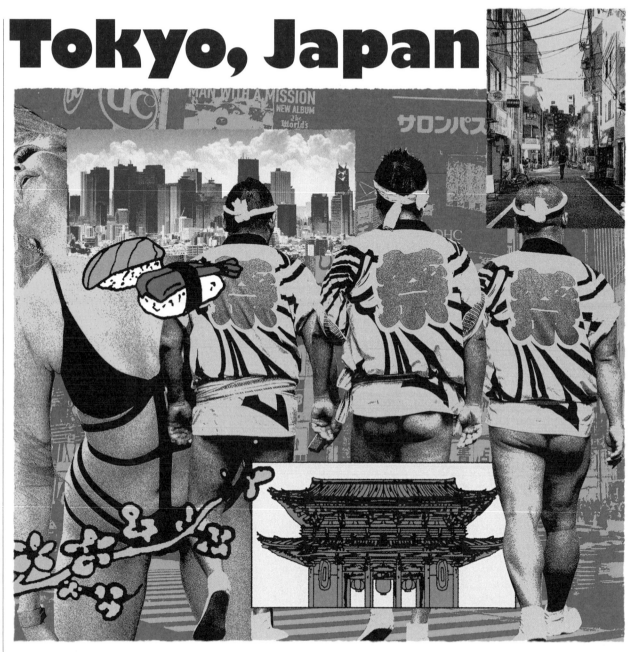

Tokyo's gayborhood, Shinjuku Ni-chōme, is home to one of the world's highest concentrations of queer and queer-friendly bars, clubs, saunas, massage parlors, and "cruising boxes" (*hattenba*). There are estimated to be more than 300 LGBTQ establishments in the area, and a stroll through the neighborhood is worth it for the names of the bars alone, which include Arty Farty, Dragon Men, Campy! Bar, and Suck'd Glory, to list just a few. There is truly something for everyone in Shinjuku, but with so many options it can be overwhelming (check out our flowchart on pages 196–97 to help you plan your evening!). In addition, queer party promoters have helped spawn a more modern clubbing scene in Tokyo, with events like BUFF and Goddess attracting hundreds of people.

Kye Koh, Japanese Party Machine

Kye Koh is originally from Osaka but is now based in Tokyo, where he throws some of Japan's biggest LGBTQ parties with the company he founded, Rainbow Events. Kye's shindigs are designed to appeal to queers of all stripes. They include his circuit party VITA, his fetish party BUFF, and his lesbian party Goddess.

Sassy Planet: What's the LGBTQ scene like in Tokyo?
Kye Koh: Most Japanese people are not out. So, that's something very different from New York or other big Western cities. In Asia, I'd say cities like Taipei and Bangkok are more open than Tokyo. But Chinese and Korean cities are less open than Tokyo. Also, the gay bars in Japan are all very small.

SP: There are a few hundred tiny gay bars in Tokyo, right?
KK: Yes. Some bars are literally a counter only that can have, like, up to five people. Shinjuku Ni-chōme is the biggest gay town in Japan, and that has hundreds of small gay bars. I'm more of a clubbing person than a bar person, so my favorite places are clubs or what they call "DJ bars." The popular clubs are Arty Farty, Dragon Men, AiSOTOPE LOUNGE, and Eagle Tokyo Blue.

SP: You throw three main parties—VITA, BUFF, and Goddess—with your company, Rainbow Events. How did you get into being a party promoter in Tokyo?
KK: I was a longtime club kid—

since high school. I love clubbing, and when I first went to a gay party in Tokyo it was a shocking experience. I'm originally from Osaka, and though I went to a small gay club there as a teenager, [my] first gay party

in Tokyo was very different. Osaka is a smaller city, so people are more closeted. They were dancing, but not really liberating themselves.

SP: When did you move to Tokyo?
KK: When I went to university. At Tokyo's gay parties, people were having so much fun, they were

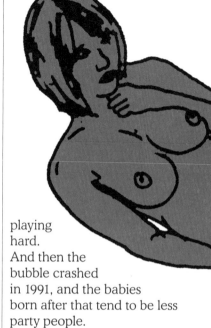

really enjoying themselves. And that's when I felt from the bottom of my heart that it is okay to be gay. Looking back, the reason I'm doing these parties is that I want to give that experience to those who are troubled with their own sexualities.

SP: You've been in Tokyo since college. How have you seen the city's LGBTQ scene change over the years?
KK: Well, my university days were 30 years ago. After that, the Internet emerged,

and that changed the scene very much. In short, not so many people go out anymore. I also think people used to be more into music. But now, the whole culture is more superficial, [and people want] instant visuals. They don't take time to listen to music. So fewer and fewer people are going to clubs, and many clubs in Tokyo have closed.

Another major change is that Tokyo's Pride has been much bigger for the past five to six years, with huge corporations joining it, and society in general is more accepting of LGBTQ people. They have learned that we exist and that they have to care about us.

SP: Why do you think people are going out less? Have apps like Grindr taken over?
KK: Yes. But I think more people still go out clubbing in other places, like Singapore and Hong Kong. Japan is at an older phase of a country's growth. We had the best economy around the late 1980s, and that's when people were working hard and

playing hard. And then the bubble crashed in 1991, and the babies born after that tend to be less party people.

Singapore's economy is at its best, and Hong Kong's economy is better than Japan's too. The youngsters there are more fun-loving. Japan's youngsters in the past few decades were more forced to save money and prepare for when they get old.

LGBTQ Tokyo Parties Organized by Kye Koh's Rainbow Events

Goddess:
"This party is for the lesbians. It's a small party of around 80 to 100 people. The music is R&B, hip-hop, EDM, and pop. Goddess is for ladies and trans women only—we accept no cis men, so even I'm not there when the Goddess party is going on."

VITA:
"This is a big club party with uplifting house music that attracts roughly 350 to 400 people. We have international guest DJs from the world's biggest circuit parties. Usually it's two floors, with the sub-floor sometimes being a transgender or lesbian party. We do it six times a year, with occasional pool parties."

BUFF:

"This is a much smaller party than VITA. It's for those who are into fetish—it's erotic and fetishy. Music-wise, BUFF has recently featured techno and house."

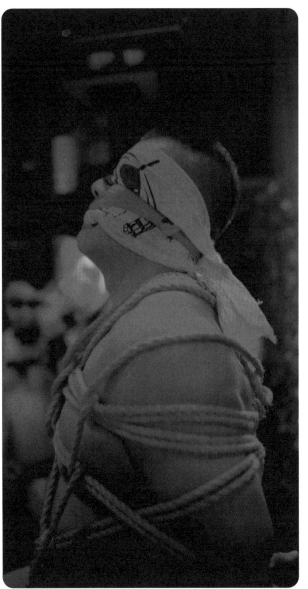

Plan Your Queer Evening in Shinjuku, Land of 300+ Gay Bars

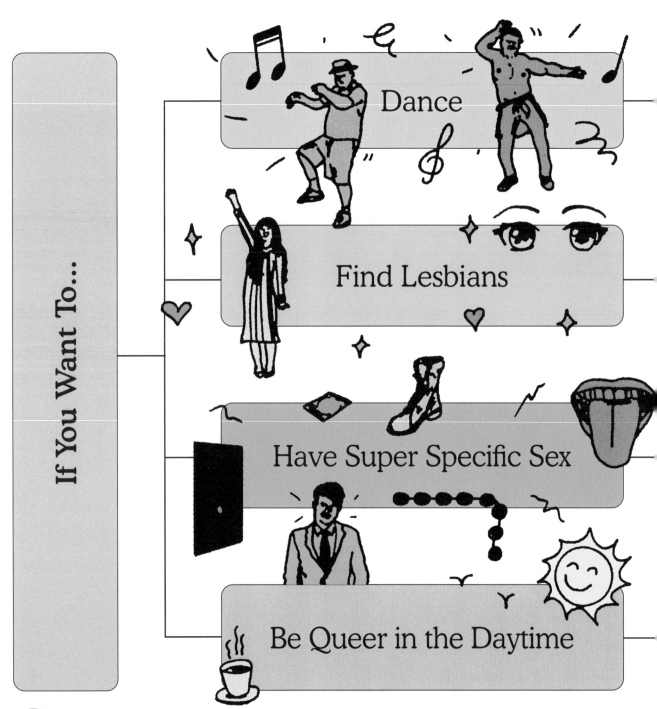

If You Want To...

Dance

Find Lesbians

Have Super Specific Sex

Be Queer in the Daytime

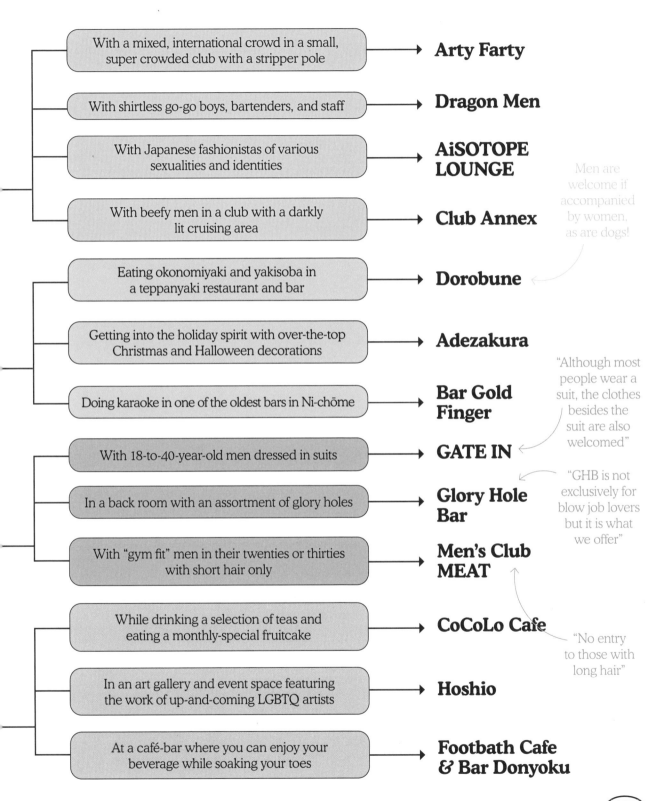

With a mixed, international crowd in a small, super crowded club with a stripper pole → **Arty Farty**

With shirtless go-go boys, bartenders, and staff → **Dragon Men**

With Japanese fashionistas of various sexualities and identities → **AiSOTOPE LOUNGE**

With beefy men in a club with a darkly lit cruising area → **Club Annex**

Men are welcome if accompanied by women, as are dogs!

Eating okonomiyaki and yakisoba in a teppanyaki restaurant and bar → **Dorobune**

Getting into the holiday spirit with over-the-top Christmas and Halloween decorations → **Adezakura**

Doing karaoke in one of the oldest bars in Ni-chōme → **Bar Gold Finger**

"Although most people wear a suit, the clothes besides the suit are also welcomed"

With 18-to-40-year-old men dressed in suits → **GATE IN**

In a back room with an assortment of glory holes → **Glory Hole Bar**

"GHB is not exclusively for blow job lovers but it is what we offer"

With "gym fit" men in their twenties or thirties with short hair only → **Men's Club MEAT**

While drinking a selection of teas and eating a monthly-special fruitcake → **CoCoLo Cafe**

"No entry to those with long hair"

In an art gallery and event space featuring the work of up-and-coming LGBTQ artists → **Hoshio**

At a café-bar where you can enjoy your beverage while soaking your toes → **Footbath Cafe & Bar Donyoku**

Kaz Senju Gives a Peek Inside Shinjuku's Living Room Bars

For the past few years, Kaz Senju, a Brooklyn-based photographer, has been documenting Shinjuku Ni-chōme through interviews and photographs. His experience with Tokyo's famous queer neighborhood goes back to the 1980s, when he first ventured there as a young gay student.

Sassy Planet: Tell us about your work documenting the queer bars in Shinjuku.
Kaz Senju: Over the past few years, I've been interviewing gay and lesbian bar owners in Shinjuku Ni-chōme, the second district of Shinjuku [ni means "2"]. Shinjuku Ni-chōme is the LGBTQ center of Japan. I've been wandering around this area since 1984. Shinjuku isn't necessarily a residential area but more of a transit city. It's one of 23 wards (similar to boroughs) in Tokyo.

SP: How long has the area been gay?
KS: For a long time, Shinjuku Ni-chōme had a special function as a prostitution district. Many of the buildings in Ni-chōme are extremely small. Before it became a gay area, it was designed as a red-light district, known as *yūkaku*. Each building consisted of a small doorway and seating area at street level where male clients could look in and negotiate the price with a manager, often an older lady, then walk upstairs with a prostitute. Originally the upstairs was just large enough to have one futon to sleep on but nothing else. They were called *kashi-zashiki*, or "rental rooms," so technically clients were paying to rent a small bed space—without mentioning what else was happening there. This is the main reason many of the gay and lesbian bars now are extremely small and only seat five to ten customers.

Clients used to be able to see the prostitute herself before negotiating the price with the manager, but having real women became illegal in 1921, [so this was] replaced with a photo of the woman in the doorway. This tradition continues today at some gay bars, where you can sometimes find "today's bartender" photos outside the bar. [In the past,] most gay and lesbian bars had no signs outside, but only a door saying "members only" to avoid random straight people walking in.

SP: How would the gays find the bars then? Just word of mouth?
KS: Before the Internet, there used to be secret maps of gay bars at the back of gay magazines, listing different bars, but it was extremely hard to find what you were looking for. Shinjuku survived the Great Kanto Earthquake of 1923 and

(1)

(2)

prospered as the only remaining red-light area after the quake in Tokyo, but it completely burned down during the Second World War. As the war ended, it was quickly rebuilt in its original shape as a red-light district for college students and salarymen [white-collar employees].

Its character was unchanged until 1958, when the government formally announced prostitution

to be illegal. As the government shut down the brothels, [they were] slowly and quietly replaced by gay and lesbian bars during the 1960s and 1970s. Ni-chōme became the largest concentration of gay and lesbian bars in the world, now hosting several hundred bars in this small area. Most of the bars are small, and the bartenders are usually also the owner of the business. People call him or her "mama."

SP: How did you first learn about Shinjuku Ni-chōme?
KS: From a gay magazine that I picked up when I was 16. Growing up in the countryside and not knowing any other gay person, I dreamt about being there and meeting my type of gay men. I entered university in

(4)

Yokohama to study architecture. It was more than an hour on the local train from my apartment to Shinjuku, but I decided to visit Shinjuku in the fall of 1984. It was a Saturday afternoon.

Without having a map, I followed my instinct and walked around. I found one café, and the owner immediately knew what I was looking for. Most of the bars don't open until late—8pm or 9pm—so the owner recommended that I to go to a bar called Zip Bar that was open early in the afternoon. When I pushed open the heavy door to Zip Bar, I met Mickey, the owner. After chatting with him for a few hours, Mickey asked me to work at the bar. I didn't know how to mix drinks but I started the following weekend at another, smaller bar Mickey owned, where I was introduced to his regular clients: artist friends, fashion designers, doctors, scientists, college professors, actors, engineers. A whole new set of friends that I didn't expect.

1: A bar decorated to celebrate the neighborhood's annual Rainbow Week. 2: The scene at Dragon. 3: Naka-dori Street in Shinjuku Ni-chōme. 4: Fujio, owner of Cream bar.

(3)

(1)

My dad is 89 years old and still runs his bar business. He is called "master" as he's the owner of the nightclub, and my mom was the mama, or queen, of our nightclub. There were two trans women who worked at my dad's club during the 1970s, and I clearly remember my first encounter with them. They were called *josou*, or cross-dressers, as well as *okama*, for a male homosexual or transvestite. They identified themselves as *okama* with a sense of pride and humor.

Katsumi was one of the trans women who worked at my dad's

That was more than 30 years ago, and Ni-chōme has continued to change since then. Most of the bars I knew are gone, replaced by new businesses. Many of my friends are gone, including Mickey. But there are a few old

(2)

places still standing. At one bar I even have my "bottle-keep," or my own spot for a bottle of gin.

SP: What are the bars like?
KS: Gay and lesbian bars in Shinjuku Ni-chōme are like a very small personal living room. You're surrounded by friends, and many of the regulars will become part of an extended

family. But bars are also theaters. It allows the proprietor or mama, as well as their clients, to dress up and be a star for a night. There's a fascinating relationship between bars in Shinjuku Ni-chōme and theater, beyond produced drag shows. Theaters used to be key communal spaces, just like gay bars, for novice men to encounter homosexual acts.

SP: What made you want to start documenting Tokyo's bar scene?
KS: My personal involvement with the bar scene goes far back to when I was young, when my parents ran a nightclub business.

(3)

(4)

club. Around age 10, I used to practice judo near my dad's place. After practice, I would stop by the club, open the door, and walk into the club, where a dozen women were in nice clothes with heavy makeup, [the air] full of perfume, serving drinks to male clients. They would come around the front desk and greet me. Katsumi was

(5)

the one who always tried to hug me, and I remember she had a five o'clock shadow even with heavy makeup. I overheard my parents' conversation about her and found out she was a trans woman, or *okama*.

A few years later I started to realize my own sexuality, my interest toward men, and my first thought was of Katsumi, *okama*, trans woman. I didn't want to become her, to be homo or *okama*, so I rejected my desire and kept that feeling deep inside. About the same time, my parents were going through a tough time in their marriage. It was a well-known fact in our family that dad tried many of the waitresses before he hired them. Mom couldn't trust anyone who worked with her at the bar. One day, I came home and she was crying in our living room. There was Katsumi holding mom's hand and trying to comfort her. As a trans woman, Katsumi was the only person who didn't compete with my mom for my dad's

(7)

attention. She was the only one with whom my mom could be honest. I was no longer afraid of being *okama*, being homo.

(6)

1: The back street Shin-Chidorigai. 2: The scene at Bar And. 3: Toru. 4: Aki at Bar Penguin. 5. Bunta, owner of Bar PROP. 6. Outside Campy! Bar on Naka-dori Street. 7: The scene at Bar OUT. Next spread: Meili Mu at Bar Zairu.

昭和Groovin!!

information

ボトルキープの期間は
3ヶ月
とさせていただきます。

佳　　　　日本舞踊

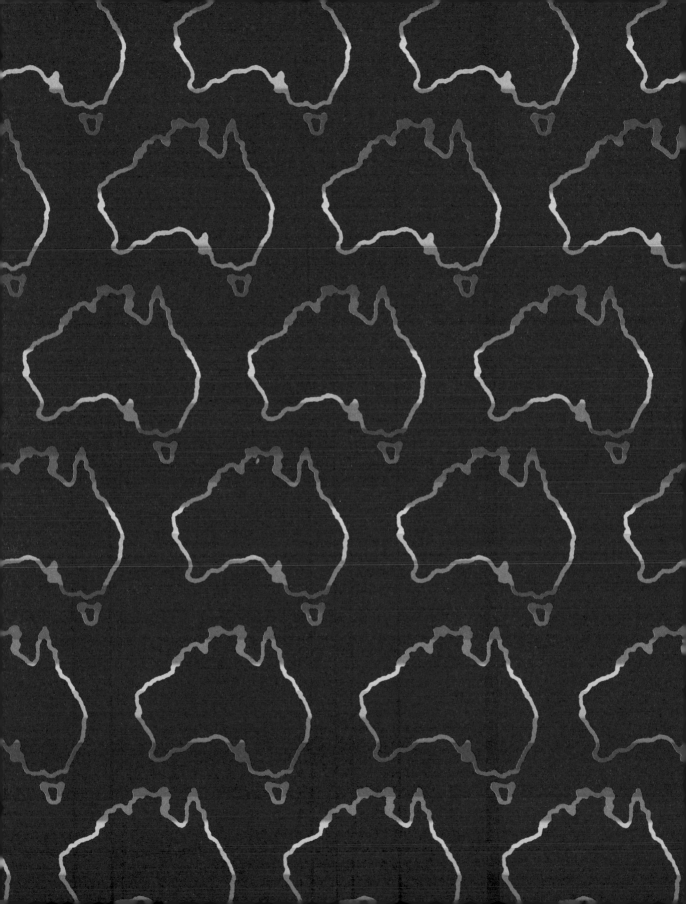

Melbourne, Victoria

elbourne is often overlooked by queer travelers eager to experience Australia's crown jewel of gay celebrations: Sydney's infamous Gay & Lesbian Mardi Gras. However, this city of 5 million has many super shiny, super gay gems of its own that make it well worth a visit. The Collingwood neighborhood is Melbourne's main LGBTQ area, but queer bars, clubs, and businesses are spread throughout the city.

The Laird, Melbourne's "Male-Only" Gay Hotel and Bar

The Laird, a hotel and bar in Melbourne, was built in 1847 and has been gay-owned and operated since the 1980s. Once the venue went queer, the surrounding community took issue with the bar's new clientele—but they apparently had no problem with its popularity among gamblers and gangsters, including the notorious (and adorably named) Squizzy Taylor. To address their concerns, The Laird was split into two: the front area was maintained as a safe space for mobsters to relax and live their best lives, while the back area was taken over by the gays.

In 1998, the bar made headlines when it was granted "male-only" status by the local government as a way to recognize its history within the gay community (particularly those of the bear and leather persuasions). "Retaining our male-only status is something we hold very dear," says Brett Lasham, co-owner of The Laird. "It helps to create the intimate and 'underground' feel of the venue, as opposed to a come-one-come-all feel."

Though the bar remains "male-only," Brett is quick to point out that this term now specifically includes all male-identifying people. "It wasn't until around 2015 that we really started to drop the whole 'masculine' theme and wording of our events," he says. "Once you accept that being male doesn't mean you need to act masculine, it takes away a lot of the toxicity that goes with the butch-versus-femme conversation." Brett already knew that many trans men were visiting the bar, and that cis male patrons had no right to deny them entry into the fold. "We were able to educate a lot of cis guys along the way, and now it just really isn't an issue," he explains.

Like many cities, the LGBTQ scene in Melbourne has changed a lot over the years; Brett says the "heyday" of queer Melbourne

Mingling at The Laird.

lasted from the 1990s through the mid-2000s. "Commercial Road in South Yarra was this big gay street, and there were huge warehouse parties in the Docklands area," he describes. Today, only a few queer-owned businesses from that era have survived, and the majority of those are on the north side, where The Laird is located. The overall scene may be smaller than it used to be, but Melbourne's leather community is "just as strong as ever," Brett says, which in turn has helped pave the way for an emerging community that The Laird also plays host to: "The rubber scene has exploded over the last four years."

Spiro Economopoulos of the Melbourne Queer Film Festival

Spiro Economopoulos is the program director for the Melbourne Queer Film Festival, which was founded in 1991 and happens for 12 days each March. The festival started small, in the back room of the bookstore Hares & Hyenas, but since then has turned into one of the leading international queer film festivals.

Sassy Planet: Tell us about yourself and your city.
Spiro Economopoulos: I grew up in Melbourne. My parents were Greek migrants who came to Australia about 60 years ago. There's a huge Greek population here—the largest outside Athens, actually. My main gig is with the Melbourne Queer Film Festival.

Melbourne is a very multicultural city. It's also more of an art-minded city in the context of Australia as a whole. People always joke that Melbournians wear black all the time. People talk about Sydney having a big LGBT scene, but Melbourne's is pretty different, pretty alternative. I'd say Sydney's queer scene is more classic in comparison.

Melbourne is definitely not an obvious city for a tourist, in terms of what to do or where things are—it's the sort of place that unfolds for you while you're here, like Los Angeles. The more time you spend here, the more you like it. It's an under-the-surface sort of place. When you're visiting Melbourne, while it's a very pretty city to look at, you still need recommendations for what to do because things here aren't very obvious.

SP: What's the Melbourne Queer Film Festival like?
SE: It's one of the oldest LGBTI film festivals in the southern hemisphere. We just celebrated our 30th anniversary. I've been there for about five years now. As the program director, I choose the films and lead the creative vision for the festival. It's the second-largest film festival in the city, and its fan base is great. The queer community here is really supportive of it. We get a few international guests each year, and people come in from all over Australia during the 12 days of the festival. It's quite extensive. It happens in March, usually, and we've started doing a mini festival in October as well, called MQFF eXtra.

(1)

SP: What are your favorite queer parties in Melbourne?
SE: There's a night called Mary which is really fun. Their tagline is that it's a "gay-ass disco"—it's a hedonistic throwback to the era of gay men's discos. You go to the front door and someone gives you a bottle of amyl [poppers] as you walk in. That happens in my neighborhood, Collingwood. There's also a weekly party called Honcho Disko. That party is a great example of the queer scene here being alternative. It's got drag, but it's weird, sort of alternative drag; it's like club kids doing drag. It's really fun.

1: Honcho Disko.

Spiro Economopoulos's
Top Melbourne To-Dos for Ho-Mos

Check out the laneways

"These are our alleyways—Melbourne has taken it to the next level, with tons of cool bars, shops, and graffiti. There's a really great culture around them; they've become really interesting spots."

Go record shopping

"There are amazing record shops all over the city."

Visit Collingwood

"It was originally a very working-class neighborhood. It's pretty gentrified now, but it's still got a nice mix of people. It's really vibrant. Restaurants, bars, cafés."

Visit the Australian Centre for the Moving Image

"ACMI is an amazing cultural center, museum, cinema, and event space."

Drink coffee

"We're the biggest coffee snobs in the world. The coffee here is incredible."

BARBA PARTY

BARBA PARTY is an "all-inclusive, sex-positive queer event" that happens monthly in Melbourne and Sydney. According to its website, the party is run by queer people of color and showcases "some of the finest queer talent and techno from Australia."

(1)

Sassy Planet: What's the vibe at BARBA PARTY, what's the music like, and what type of person usually goes?
BARBA PARTY: It's a sex-positive queer event. We see BARBA as a place of healing that will have you sweating out your demons in an open and inclusive safe space.

The BARBA family is a multitalented and diverse crew. BARBA is a bridge that brings together different parts of our community. Our guests are anyone looking to spend a whole night dancing to techno and breaking free from their routines and mainstream spaces.

SP: What makes the scene at BARBA unique from other LGBTQ parties in Melbourne?
BP: Actually, the Melbourne scene is very unique itself. It's progressive, alternative, and diverse. It's really strong in general, so the best part is that we're not competing with other parties. It's all about respect, and creating as many spaces and experiences as we can. We see these events as one of many ways for queers to find each other and connect, so having many different vibes for people to explore is important. It's a truly collaborative scene, and we're always cheering on our fellow promoters and artists, whether they be mainstays or emergent.

SP: How has BARBA evolved since it began?
BP: Five years ago, BARBA PARTY became one of the first places where queers in Melbourne could enjoy a well-curated underground techno party, inspired by the club scenes of Bogotá and Berlin.

Over time, BARBA found its own identity, showcasing installations, performance art, and immersive designs as well as the hottest DJs. We've been honored to showcase some of Melbourne's most boundary-pushing artists while also hosting some of our favorite international queers, like Roi Perez, Nastia Reigel, and Casey Spooner. We like to

(2)

curate the night so that people see something a little different every time and get exposed to artists they may not normally look for, or dance to music they might not normally listen to. We aim to be a place of discovery, whether that is something external, within yourself, or both. At BARBA, people from all different backgrounds, of every age, any gender or sexuality, and any locale, become one big ecosystem of sweat, bass, and freedom.

Another aspect that makes BARBA different is that we're dedicated to creating conversations around mental health, harm reduction, drugs, body positivity, and sex positivity in our community. When the BARBA Babes (that's how we refer to our patrons) come to BARBA, they don't know what to expect, but they're all ready for a wild ride. We don't have a formula, and every night has a different atmosphere. We just put together the ingredients that intrigue and excite us, with a goal to create a night where everyone gets to connect and express themselves and celebrate each other.

(3)

SP: What's the queer scene generally like in Melbourne?

BP: The Melbourne scene has been evolving and growing so fast in recent years, from the old-school gay bars and pubs to unique and niche underground clubs, and illegal warehouse or outdoor events. Throughout the year Melbournians and travelers alike can enjoy many different types of festivals, live events, and a vibrant queer performing arts scene.

Melbourne is the true arts capital of Australia. It's been the cultural capital of Australia for a while, recognized internationally as such. Many queer artists come to Melbourne from afar to carve their space, especially if they're

from more conservative areas. It's a city with a huge movement of all kinds of artistic expression, underpinned by its welcoming atmosphere.

SP: What would you recommend a first-time LGBTQ visitor do when they come to Melbourne?

BP: No matter your personal preference, you'll find something to cater to your tastes. If you're looking for a filthy club night with extra sex, hit TROUGH X or FANTASTIC. For vibrant and bubbly fun, hit up UMAMI or Unicorns. Want some alternative drag? Then stroll down to Honcho Disko on Thursday night or seek out amazing shows like YUMMY or Hear No Evil.

If you don't know what you feel like, simply wandering the streets of Collingwood, Fitzroy, or Brunswick will provide you with street art, great food, and beautiful queers. Melbourne is a city that rewards the curious traveler. Go with the flow and you might just find the perfect party hidden at the end of a laneway. Don't be too shy to ask a local for advice.

1-3: Images from BARBA PARTY's inclusive, sex-positive queer events.

(1)

(2)

Hares & Hyenas

While most LGBTQ bookstores—which used to be a gay staple in major cities across the world—have gone extinct, Hares & Hyenas, located off Brunswick Street in Melbourne's Spanishtown, is still going strong. The store, founded in 1991, offers LGBTQ fiction, non-fiction, erotica, and magazines—truly a one-stop shop for all your reading needs!

Since its beginnings, the bookstore has worked to eschew the gay/lesbian binary. "The concept of 'queer' as an umbrella identity started bubbling in the background around this time," says Crusader Hillis, who co-founded the store along with Rowland Thomson. "It was first noticeable to us in comics and cartoons and the independent and fringe publications we carried."

Crusader and Rowland have also ensured that the titles they stock are inclusive for everyone. "We recognized that [the shop] needed to provide material for adventurous heterosexuals, and for any straight people wanting to buy books on sexuality," explains Crusader. "Right up to this day there's little in general bookstores that covers sexuality for people." At Hares & Hyenas you can find "sex manuals on kink, disability, and aging," among other things, "as well as a large number of books on things such as anal sex, cunnilingus, sex toys, and polyamory for straight people. Those remain a very popular part of our bookshop's offer," Crusader says. The store also carries over 70 titles on donor and assisted reproductive technology (ART). "We're the only bookshop in Australia to specialize in ART and diverse family structures," he says. "We even carry a book set within a poly family."

In 2007, the store opened a café. Then, in 2012, they launched a fully licensed performance venue called (what else?) the Hare Hole. Typically, the space hosts three shows a week that range from poetry nights to comedy shows. "Our contact with performers over the years has provided us [access to] some of the most accomplished mid-career artists in Australia, alongside a busy program of emerging artists who welcome the professional presentation standards, marketing support, and unique atmosphere of the venue," Crusader says. "It's cherished by many artists and we are highly regarded across the arts sector."

As queer businesses, from bookstores to nightclubs, continue to shutter around the globe, how has Hares & Hyenas managed to stay afloat? Crusader explains that, back in the 1990s, "There was a stampede towards opening gay and lesbian businesses, but there was also a lack of skill underlying many endeavors. Nothing sealed a gay coffee shop's fate faster than the failure to produce barista-quality coffee to Melbourne's discerning poofs and other coffee snobs." Knowing what their audience wants is what has kept Hares & Hyenas going. In terms of queer bookstores specifically, Crusader says that, in many ways, it was their success around the world that led to their downfall: "Large chain bookstores, most of which are now long since broke, began coveting queer readers to such a degree that, in order to attract them, many took losses on book sales in this sector."

Hares & Hyenas has also survived, Crusader posits, because they have refused to pigeonhole their business as one that caters exclusively to gay men. "In Melbourne we lost many customers to Borders as it colonized our two main areas, South Yarra and Carlton/Fitzroy—but most [of them] were well-heeled homosexual men who always felt Hares & Hyenas had a tinge of the unwashed radical about it. Our customer base was predicated on a much wider [group] than lesbians and gay men, and it was during this time that we first saw strong community support from the many marginalized communities we represented on our shelves."

1 & 2: The bookstore also houses a café and bar, and hosts events.

Sydney, New South Wales

Sydney is home to some creatively named gay bars (see: The Bearded Tit, the Slyfox, and The Imperial Erskineville). It's also home to the infamous Sydney Gay & Lesbian Mardi Gras, which takes place on the first Saturday in March each year and is one of the world's largest LGBTQ Pride events. In February 2014, the city's infamous nightlife scene suffered a major blow when conservative politicians introduced "lockout laws" that required venues to cut off admittance at 1:30am and to stop serving drinks at 3am. But in 2019, the laws were relaxed and queer nightlife bounced back with a vengeance, with an insane number of bars, parties, saunas, clubs, and more to choose from.

Kat Dopper is Proudly "Heaps Gay"

Kat Dopper is the founder of Heaps Gay, a queer party whose name is a play on a derogatory Aussie term. Beyond reclaiming an offensive expression, the aim is to create a space that resembles a house party—inclusive, relaxed, and welcoming to all types of queer and queer-adjacent people.

Sassy Planet: Tell us about yourself and your city.
Kat Dopper: G'day! I'm a girl from central New South Wales who now lives in the Sydney suburb of Newtown. It took me nearly 30 years to work out that I was queer. As a kid I was drawn to the Big Smoke and would sometimes catch the train all the way down to Sydney's bohemian heart, the Inner West, to watch all the strange and fabulous people going about their days. When I was 17, some friends and I travelled to watch the Mardi Gras parade for the first time. I remember so clearly standing on a milk crate drinking a shitty warm beer and thinking to myself that I'd never seen something so wonderful.

It wasn't until years later, while living in London, that I fell in love with my best friend and realized that I was a flaming homosexual. While it was totally unrequited, I wouldn't change a thing about the experience, and I've never looked back! I love my queer friends and family, and I'm so thankful that I spend my days working toward the greater queer good: our right to dance and have a good time!

SP: Why did you decide to start Heaps Gay?
KD: When I returned to Sydney in my late twenties, I was a horny queer looking for somewhere that my friends (some straight, some not) and I could go out and party—somewhere I could pash a girl on the dancefloor and my friends could feel welcome. Basically, I wanted to find Sydney's version of London's [now-defunct gay pub] George & Dragon. I soon realized that a regular all-inclusive party didn't exist in Sydney at that time. I couldn't get over my need to share a dancefloor with queer and queer-adjacent people of all persuasions, and so Heaps Gay was born.

SP: How did you come up with that name?
In 2013, the term "heaps gay" was being used around Australia as a negative term—a means of saying, "that's heaps weird and heaps shit!" My friends and I weren't sure how well it would be received by queer people, who might not be comfy with reclaiming the term, but when I held the first event, at a run-down pub called The Gladstone, it was

A Heaps Gay party at Manning Bar.

(1)

incredible! It was jam-packed full of the most gorgeous and diverse queer people that I'd ever seen in one place in Sydney.

From that first party to now, the aim has always been to create a space that feels like a house party. Whether we're holding a warehouse party in Marrickville, a street party in Sydenham, or a queer ball at the city's iconic Town Hall, the vibe is always all-inclusive, no judgments, just raging good times. If you're open-minded, open-hearted, and you like to party, then you're welcome. We don't have resident DJs or book the same acts again and again. When you come to a Heaps Gay event, you never know what you're going to get! You might see Cakes da Killa, Ngaiire, Vanessa Amorosi, Electric Fields, Touch Sensitive, Dorian Electra, or Le1f; or you might see an incredible queer person performing to a crowd for the first time. We also love

to activate the city, so you won't see Heaps Gay at the same venue very often.

SP: What's the legendary Sydney Mardi Gras like?

KD: Sydney Gay & Lesbian Mardi Gras is one of the world's largest LGBTQIA art festivals. The legends at Mardi Gras know how passionate I am about ensuring that queer culture in Sydney (and around Australia) thrives, and they invited me to be the creative director of the 2020 festival season—what a privilege! This included directing all creative aspects of the southern hemisphere's biggest queer celebration: 17 days and nights, including the world-famous night parade and party.

Today, hundreds of thousands of people participate in the Mardi Gras festival. Not all of those people understand that Mardi Gras started as a protest. Inspired by the Stonewall riots

in the US, a small collective of brave Australian people took to the streets in 1978 for the first Mardi Gras parade. This quickly descended into harassment and violence at the hands of police, and many of those who took to the streets to demand equal rights were arrested.

Over the years, the march has evolved into a celebration, but personally I think it's critical that the festival continues to shine a light on inequalities here in Australia and in the Asia-Pacific region. I think Sydney Mardi Gras can be both a pride parade and a protest.

I think the challenge for Mardi Gras is to continue to remain relevant and accessible for all kinds of queer people, of all ages. Mardi Gras is a beacon of hope for many people around the country and the region. The parade provides visibility that

(2)

can frankly be life-changing for the many queer young people growing up in small towns who lack support. I hope that Mardi Gras will continue their great work for many, many years to come.

(3)

SP: What makes the lesbian/ queer women's scene in Sydney unique? Does it exist harmoniously with the gay men's scene?

KD: Our scene has become way more diverse in the last five to ten years, with a disruption of the segregation of gay and lesbian bars, which personally I love!

When I was younger there was Oxford Street in Darlinghurst, the big gay strip where Sydney's first gay clubs opened up in 1969— clubs like ARQ, The Stonewall Hotel, Midnight Shift, The Oxford Hotel. Think big, banging dancefloors and gay men as far as the eye can see. Lesbian bars were smaller and more unassuming, but nonetheless there were always a few good options each month. While the gay scene is alive and well in Sydney, there are only a handful of lesbian events left, and no lesbian bars.

In 2014, the city introduced lockout laws that prevented patrons from accessing venues late at night. These laws, combined with gentrification, have contributed to a massive loss of late-night culture around the city, including the permanent closure of over 170 music venues. But you know what? You can't keep people down! The last few years have seen a burst in new events striving to make sure there are places to party. I think many of these newer events are also trying to disrupt the idea that you can only party with people who identify in the same way that you do. Some of my favorite regular parties include House of Mince, Honcho Disko and Unicorns [both of which happen in

Own Nudes, an undie party that celebrates body positivity; Bear Bar; and community-led vogue balls run by queer people of color.

SP: What are your thoughts on the closure of lesbian bars worldwide?

KD: The closure of lesbian bars around the globe sucks! There are currently no lesbian bars or clubs in Sydney. I feel there are many factors as to why lesbian bars are no longer a thing, from

(4)

Melbourne too], Queerbourhood, and ongoing queer venues like The Red Rattler, The Imperial Hotel, Universal, and The Bearded Tit.

There are other events in our scene that celebrate diversity and generate their own unique subcultures, which I think is so special: events like Leak Your

gentrification to venue and bar owners realizing that running spaces that are welcoming of all sexualities and cultural backgrounds makes for a more

1: A Heaps Gay party.
2: Heaps Gay Street Festival.
3 & 4: Sydney Gay & Lesbian Mardi Gras.

profitable business. And perhaps it's also generational. Young people are growing up not caring about labels—and our fight for inclusion and equality has also meant the erasure of lesbian spaces, sadly.

SP: Do you have any tidbits of Sydney lesbian history to share?
KD: Friends are always telling me stories about how great the '90s were in Sydney and how drag king culture was huge. Half my pals were the famous kings at that time: John Dark, The Kingpins, D-Vinyl. Parties like Kingki Kingdom and Girlesque ran weekly competitions, and the scene was thriving. In the past decade, king culture hasn't really existed, but today in Sydney it's making a comeback—monthly dedicated parties are popping up, and I'm excited about the resurgence.

SP: What are your fave queer women's parties in Sydney?
KD: Kooky is my fave, it's an institution! It's been going strong in Sydney since the mid-1990s. Events happen every three months or so and are really magical. It's a chance for older clubbers and newfound queers to come together on the dancefloor. I've only just found my place here as I've grown into my queerness, and I'm grateful for the experiences.

Also, House of Mince is a queer collective that throws a weekly Sunday party called Pavlova Bar. It's a debaucherous, hedonistic sweatbox that some say is Sydney's Berghain— without the sex on premises.

(1)

(2)

1 & 2: Sydney Gay & Lesbian Mardi Gras.

Kat Dopper's
Top Sydney To-Dos
for Ho-Mos

Newtown

"Start your day here and swing past The Stinking Bishops and P&V Merchants to pick up some cheese and natural wine, and then head for a picnic and naked swim at Little Congwong Beach, or to the ladies' baths in Coogee if swimwear is more your thing."

Zoo Emporium

"Head back to the city via Surry Hills and visit Zoo Emporium for all your sparkly, colorful retro-vintage needs. It's owned by renowned queer artist Emma Price, who was a member of the legendary all-female artist collective The Kingpins back in the 1990s."

Queer-run restaurants

"After an afternoon nap, throw on those sparkles and head to dinner at Bloodwood or BART Jr, both queer-owned and queer-run restaurants. So delish."

The Bearded Tit

"After dinner, swing past The Bearded Tit for a drink and dance. It's the queerest neighborhood bar, you can't miss it while you're in Sydney. It feels like you're in a friend's lounge, with wall-mounted animals, knitted vulvas, and free hugs."

Palms on Oxford

"Go here late, and get ready to dance like no one is watching: it's a shit dive bar with bad lighting, full of people belting out ballads from the 1980s and pop bangers from the 2000s."

Harish Bhandari is an overdancer who is gradually working on "Museum Gift Shop Lady," a photo essay honoring those who support the arts through shopping. Born in London, raised in California, and living in Brooklyn since 2004, he has traveled extensively for both work and fun, always curious to learn about the up-and-coming neighborhood, underground party, or new restaurant, wherever he is.

David Dodge is a freelance writer and journalist covering travel, LGBTQ stuff, politics, culture and more for the *New York Times*, *Travel + Leisure*, *CNN Traveler*, *The Advocate*, *Glass*, *Huffington Post*, and *Luxury*, as well as other outlets. He lives in Manhattan but isn't a snob about it—some of his best friends have been to Brooklyn.

Nick Schiarizzi is a video editor and director who also co-runs SSHH, a multipurpose art and education organization based in New York City. He is a founding member of the CHERYL artist collective, through which he got to travel the world for years covered in fake blood, DJing the greatest hits of Miley Cyrus's Disney Channel era to the masses.

Bráulio Amado is a graphic designer and illustrator from Portugal, currently living in New York City. He has difficulty pronouncing the words "chair" and "cookies" in English and is continually trying not to feel insecure about it. His client list includes publications such as the *New York Times* and *New Yorker* and musicians like Frank Ocean, Róisín Murphy, Rex Orange County, and Robyn, among others.

This book never would have happened without our editor, Ali Gitlow, who had the original vision of turning our scrappy, queer little travel website into a resource you can actually hold in your hands. We are indebted to her for her foresight, and for not slut-shaming us when we proposed conducting the bulk of our research on Grindr. We also need to thank our honorary fifth bottom, a heterosexual male named Marc Linder, who bore with us through months of web design—and redesign—in order to launch our site, forbottoms.com, which provided the inspiration for this project. We will buy you that steak someday. We also thank our friends David Orton and Kevin Saunders, both of whom have suffered through countless ruined dinners featuring this project as the sole discussion topic. We also thank them for contributing many amazing ideas for the book, all of which we ignored, of course, because we didn't think of them ourselves.

Lastly, we made this book with the help of literally hundreds of individuals, who connected us to interesting LGBTQ people and things, helped us source photographs, or simply told us about queer life in their cities. This includes anyone whose name (or handle) appears in this book. But in particular we thank, from the bottoms of our hearts, the following people, whose contributions can't be topped:

Jon Arnold
Edgar Bucholtz
Gustavo Carmona
Shahar Cicelsky
Sam Clayton
Morgan Clement
Christopher Collins
El Puñal Dorao
Gary Emenitove
Christopher Gathman
Aditya Ghosh
Nizar Haraké
Samantha Hudson
Viwe Jack-Gcilishe
Dustin Koda
Jay Koneck

Michael Linington
Julian Liu
Stephanos Michaelides
Bill Pfeiffer
Anderson Porto
Vangelis Rissou
Lisa Rose
Giuseppe Saturno
Amy Schindler
Aimee Selby
Kaz Senju
Felipe Serrano
Nick Shea
Paco Tostado
Jay Tremont
Avinash Wadhwani

➤ Picture Credits

Front cover and flap: images courtesy and © Alvesgaspar; Bráulio Amado; Ankit Bhuptani; Sandra Blow; Christopher Collins; Bruno Delfino; DVSROSS; Brian Gratwicke; Lee-Roy Jason; Mari Juliano; Yazeed Kamaldien; Caldwell Linker; Victor Luque; Mike McBey; Richard Arthur Norton; Minos Ntokopoulos; Darren Nunis; Kaz Senju; tingyaoh.

Back cover and flap: images courtesy and © Bráulio Amado; Tiffany Von Arnim; Jon Arnold and Emma Kroeger; Patrick Bowland; Christopher Collins; Juliano Corbetta; Daryl Figueroa; Tan Kaninthanond; Cachorro Lozano; Etsuko Miyasaka; Mikel Ortega; Papi Boys; Kaz Senju; Tom Shockey; Suponac.

North America
Austin, Texas: images courtesy and © Austin Community College (p. 10); Tomek Baginski (p. 10); Jeremy Banks (p. 10); Julian Eternal (pp. 12, 13, 14 left and right, 15 top); Clayton Gibson (p. 15 bottom); David Ingram (p. 10); Jason Jacobs (p. 10). Chicago, Illinois: images courtesy and © Alan Light (pp. 16, 17); Tom Shockey (p. 16). Honolulu, Hawaii: images courtesy and © Dustin Koda (p. 19); Darren Nunis (pp. 18, 21 left); Daniel Ramirez (pp. 18, 21 right). Kansas City, Missouri: images courtesy and © Charvex (p. 22); Stuart Seeger (p. 22); Keith Spare (pp. 23 all images, 24). Mexico City, Mexico: images courtesy and © Sandra Blow (pp. 26, 28, 30, 31 left and right); José Guadalupe Posada (p. 27); Nick Schiarizzi

(pp. 26, 29). Miami, Florida: images courtesy and © Nichlas Andersen (p. 32); Christopher Collins (pp. 32, 34 left and right, 35, 36–37); Ryan Spencer (p. 32). Montreal, Canada: images courtesy and © Bruno Guérin (pp. 40, 41 bottom); Saad Al-Hakkak (p. 39); Nick Schiarizzi (pp. 38, 41 top); Tobias (p. 38). Nashville, Tennessee: images courtesy and © Tanner Boriack (p. 42); Eric Gilliland (p. 42); NashTrash Tours (p. 43 left); Play Dance Bar (p. 44); Christa Suppan (p. 43 middle and right). New York City, New York: images courtesy and © Bráulio Amado (pp. 46, 51, 52 left); Harish Bhandari (p. 48 bottom left); Lanee Bird (pp. 52 right, 53 top and bottom); DJ Lina Bradford (p. 49); Corey Craig (p. 50); DVSROSS (p. 46); Santiago Felipe and Ladyfag (p. 48 right); Sharon Mollerus (p. 46); Paul Sableman (p. 48 top left); Nick Schiarizzi (pp. 46, 47); May S. Young (p. 46). Omaha, Nebraska: images courtesy and © Bill Anderson (p. 57 top); Sage Griffith (p. 54); Roland Massow (p. 55); John Matychuk (p. 54); Sarah Miller (p. 56); Queer Omaha Archives (p. 54); Tony Webster (p. 57 bottom). Pittsburgh, Pennsylvania: images courtesy and © Harish Bhandari (p. 58); Ellis Garvey (p. 58); Caldwell Linker (pp. 58, 59, 61, 64 all images, 65 top and bottom); Masha MouseBones Vereshchenko (pp. 60, 63 left and right). Salt Lake City, Utah: images courtesy and © Bruno Delfino (p. 66); Garrett (p. 66); Dallas Graham (p. 66); Timothy Pearce (p. 69 right); Chris Sloan (p. 69 left); Jesse Walker (pp. 67

left and right, 68 top and bottom). San Francisco, California: images courtesy and © Cabure Bonugli (pp. 72, 75 left and right, 76 top and bottom); Aaron Kato (p. 72); Kennejima (p. 72); Dave Maass (p. 77 bottom); Mike McBey (p. 72); Oscar Pineda (p. 74); Frank Schulenburg (p. 77 top). Seattle, Washington: images courtesy and © Matt Baume (pp. 78, 79, 80 top right and bottom right, 81, 82–83, 85 right); Tyler Merbler (p. 80 left); mikeyskatie (p. 85 left); Tiffany Von Arnim (p. 78).

South America
Bogotá, Colombia: images courtesy and © Jorge Andrés Calderón (p. 91 left); Mark Chestnut (p. 88); Peter Chovanec (p. 88); Roberto Fiadone (p. 91 right); Papi Boys (pp. 88, 89); Pedro Szekely (p. 88); Theatron de Película (p. 90). Buenos Aires, Argentina: images courtesy and © Bráulio Amado (p. 92); Agustín Ceretti (pp. 93, 94 top); Irenef74 (p. 95 left); Manticora87 (p. 95 right); Poleth Rivas (p. 94 bottom); Fabio Téllez (p. 92). Salvador, Brazil: images courtesy and © Turismo Bahia (pp. 96, 97). Santiago, Chile: images courtesy and © Christian Córdova (p. 98); Fausto Discoteque (pp. 98, 99 left); m.sanhuezacelsi (p. 99 right). São Paulo, Brazil: images courtesy and © Batekoo (p. 109 top and bottom); Juliano Corbetta (pp. 100, 101 left); Mari Juliano (pp. 100, 101 right, 102–7 all images); Matt Kieffer (p. 100).

Europe
Athens, Greece: images courtesy and © Matt Kieffer (p. 112);

Minos Ntokopoulos (pp. 112, 113). Berlin, Germany: images courtesy and © Matze A. (p. 118 right); James Dennes (p. 114); Fionn Große (p. 119 left); Gunnar Klack (p. 118 left); Victor Luque (pp. 114, 117); Filip Maliković (p. 114); Nikita Pishchugin (p. 119 right). Bologna, Italy: images courtesy and © Samuele Cavadini (p. 122 bottom); Matteo Giorgi (p. 121); Richard Mortel (p. 120); SerenaPaliria Images (p. 123 left); Matteo Tasca (pp. 120, 122 top and middle); Yuri Virovets (p. 120); Вvласенко (p. 123 right). Lisbon, Portugal: images courtesy and © Alvesgaspar (p. 124); Vera Mermelo (pp. 125, 126, 127). London, UK: images courtesy and © Bráulio Amado (p. 130); Jon Arnold and Emma Kroeger (pp. 130, 134–35 all images); Kurtis Garbutt (p. 130); Stephen Isaac-Wilson (p. 131 left); It's No Game (p. 132 right); David Jones (p. 130); Benn McGuinness (p. 132 left); Ewan Munro (p. 133); Taavi Randmaa (p. 131 right). Madrid, Spain: images courtesy and © Alejandria Cinque (p. 137 top and bottom); Cachorro Lozano (p. 136); Mikel Ortega (p. 136); Eric Titcombe (p. 136). Paris, France: images courtesy and © Alexander (p. 138); Cahtls (p. 140 left); Laure Guicherd (p. 141 left); Legay Choc (p. 139); John M. (p. 138); La Mutinerie (p. 141 right); Rog01 (p. 138).

Africa

Accra, Ghana: images courtesy and © Kwabena Akuamoah-Boateng (p. 144); Muntaka Chasant (p. 144); Denis Nzioka

(p. 144). Cairo, Egypt: images courtesy and © Dan (p. 146). Cape Town, South Africa: images courtesy and © Daniels Photography (p. 149); Brian Gratwicke (p. 148); Duane Huff (p. 151 left); Yazeed Kamaldien (pp. 148, 150 top and bottom); Mike Peel (p. 151 right). Johannesburg, South Africa: images courtesy and © Lee-Roy Jason (pp. 152, 154, 156–59 all images); Nicholas Lawrence (p. 153); Media Club (p. 152); Willem van Valkenburg (p. 155). Lagos, Nigeria: images courtesy and © Harry Itie (p. 161); Omoeko Media (p. 160).

Asia

Amman, Jordan: images courtesy and © Paul Arps (p. 164); Dan Lundberg (p. 167 right); Alisa Zaira Reznick (p. 165); Jude Al Safadi (p. 167 left). Bangkok, Thailand: images courtesy and © Bráulio Amado (p. 168); Blemished Paradise (p. 168); Alejandro Cartagena (p. 168); David Dodge (p. 173 bottom); Tan Kaninthanond (p. 168); Saroj Kunatanad (pp. 169, 170–71 all images, 173 top); Bharamee Thamrongmas (p. 168). Ho Chi Minh City, Vietnam: images courtesy and © Bráulio Amado (p. 174); Karma Creatives (pp. 175, 176, 177 top and bottom). Jeddah, Saudi Arabia: images courtesy and © Daryl Figueroa (p. 178); Mohammed Hassan (p. 178); Richard Ricciardi (p. 178). Mumbai, India: images courtesy and © Ankit Bhuptani (pp. 180, 181 left and right); Durga Gawde (pp. 184, 185); Naman Koul (p. 182); Satyajeet Mazumdar (p. 180); Queer Azaadi

Mumbai (p. 183); Sid Saxena (p. 180). Taipei, Taiwan: images courtesy and © Fred Hsu (p. 189 left); Gelee Lai (p. 189 right); Kaz Senju (pp. 186, 188 top and bottom); tingyaoh (p. 186); 毛貓大少爺 (p. 186); weimingtang.org (p. 187 left and right). Tokyo, Japan: images courtesy and © Kii Chan (pp. 191, 195 all images); Etsuko Miyasaka (pp. 190, 193 all images); Louie Nicolo Nimor (p. 190); Kaz Senju (pp. 190, 198–201 all images, 202–3); UTO (p. 194 all images); Ryo Yoshitake (p. 190).

Australia

Melbourne, Victoria: images courtesy and © Patrick Bowland (p. 206); Nicholas Cole (p. 206); Joel Deveraux (p. 208 right); Sofia Fontenla/MQFF (p. 209 left); Hares & Hyenas (p. 212 top and bottom); Imago Design (pp. 210 left and right, 211); Brett Lasham (p. 207); Krista Purmale (p. 206); Zina Sofer/MQFF (p. 208 left); Annie Spratt (p. 209 right). Sydney, New South Wales: images courtesy and © Bruce Baker (pp. 217 left and right, 218 top and bottom); Peter Darnley (pp. 215 right, 216 left); Goran Has (p. 214); Ken Leanfore (p. 215 left); Satsuki Minota (p. 216 right); NomadicPics (p. 219 right); Suponac (p. 214).

© Prestel Verlag, Munich · London · New York, 2021
A member of Penguin Random House Verlagsgruppe GmbH
Neumarkter Strasse 28 · 81673 Munich

© for the text by Harish Bhandari, David Dodge, and Nick Schiarizzi, 2021
© for the photographs see Picture Credits, p. 222, 2021
© for the illustrations by Bráulio Amado, 2021

In some cases, interviews have been lightly edited for clarity.

Library of Congress Control Number: 2021930240

A CIP catalogue record for this book is available from the British Library.

Editorial direction: Ali Gitlow
Copyediting and proofreading: Aimee Selby
Design and layout: Nick Shea
Production management: Friederike Schirge
Separations: Reproline Mediateam
Printing and binding: DZS Grafik, d.o.o., Ljubljana
Paper: Tauro Offset

Penguin Random House Verlagsgruppe FSC® N001967

Printed in Slovenia

ISBN 978-3-7913-8756-7

www.prestel.com